Indians in Maryland and Delaware

BIBLIOGRAPHICAL SERIES
*The Newberry Library Center
for the History of the American Indian*

General Editor
Francis Jennings

Assistant Editor
William R. Swagerty

The Center Is Supported by Grants from

The National Endowment for the Humanities
The Ford Foundation
The W. Clement and Jessie V. Stone Foundation
The Woods Charitable Fund, Inc.
Mr. Gaylord Donnelley

Indians in Maryland and Delaware

A Critical Bibliography

FRANK W. PORTER III

Published for the Newberry Library

Indiana University Press

BLOOMINGTON AND LONDON

Manufactured in the United States of America

Library of Congress Cataloging in Publication Data

Porter, Frank W   1947–
  Indians in Maryland and Delaware.

  (Bibliographical series)
  Includes index.
    1. Indians of North America—Maryland—Bibliography. 2. Indians of North America—Delaware—Bibliography. I. Title. II. Series.
  Z1209.2.U52M376 [E78.M3] 016.9751'004'97 79–2460
  ISBN 0–253–30954–9 pbk.   1 2 3 4 5 83 82 81 80 79

CONTENTS

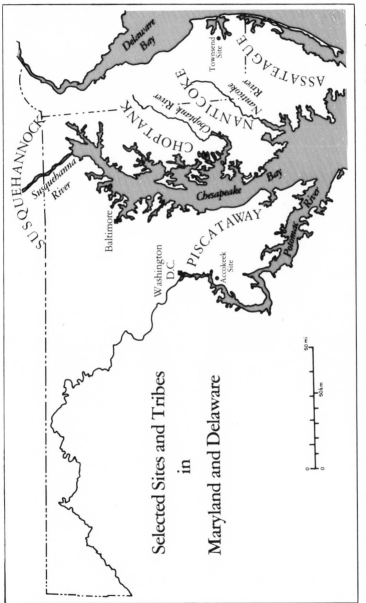

Selected Sites and Tribes
in
Maryland and Delaware

Mary Traeger, Cartographer, University of Maryland

INTRODUCTION

At the time of first European contact, the territory that is now Maryland and Delaware was inhabited by numerous Algonquian-speaking tribes. Within this broad expanse of country are a variety of major ecological zones: the Coastal Plain, rich in fish and shellfish; the Piedmont Plateau, an area of undulating hills and low ridges incised by numerous deep and narrow stream valleys; and the densely forested Blue Ridge Mountains. The Nanticokes, Piscataways, and other tribes in Maryland and Delaware possessed a sophisticated political organization with a centralized authority, had devised a variety of economic adjustments to their habitat, and were able to satisfy all their basic needs within these ecological zones by a combination of gathering, hunting, fishing, and agriculture. One of the most significant consequences stemming from the contact between these tribes and European settlers was the decline of the aboriginal population. In their efforts to accommodate the continued presence of these intruders and preserve some semblance of their traditional culture, the Indians sought legal counsel, waged war, and finally resigned themselves to reservations. All to no avail. By 1756 it was estimated that only 140 Indians remained in Maryland. Many of the smaller, lesser-known tribes had been forced to disperse and were later absorbed into other tribes; others simply vanished, leaving no evidence about their fate. In many instances tribes retreated as a result of culture contact. As early as 1722 individual families of Nanticokes began to leave Maryland. By 1748 a majority of the Nanticokes and Piscataways had migrated to the Juniata River and Wyoming Valley of Pennsylvania. At the close of the eighteenth century there was a general consensus, although it later proved inaccurate, that no Indians remained in Maryland and Delaware.

During the late nineteenth and early twentieth centuries American anthropologists and ethnologists were dedicated to salvaging the culture of the American Indian in its aboriginal state. Earnestly believing that the last stronghold of the "real" Indian lay west of the Mississippi River, many scholars and laymen held the attitude that Indians in the East either had become extinct or were so mixed genetically with Whites and Blacks that they had suffered a complete loss of their aboriginal culture and were therefore not worthy of serious study. Frank G. Speck, James Mooney, and David I. Bushnell were notable exceptions. Using questionnaires, fieldwork, and historical research, they determined the existence of several enclaves of Indian survivals in the eastern United States. Through their own efforts and those of their students, they succeeded in preserving bits and pieces of the aboriginal heritage of these groups. Most anthropologists and ethnologists, however, failed to explain the survival of these groups through the nineteenth century to the present because they had not been adequately trained to use primary historical documents or to discern the critical processes of acculturation. When several scholars finally directed their research efforts to Indians in the East, they did so with the biased assumption that they were dealing with triracial isolates—a presumed admixture of Indian, White, and Black. Although after the late 1940s interest in Indians in the East appeared to wane, with the resurgence of the Native American movement a renewed concern is being kindled about these neglected groups.

In recent years there has been a significant increase in the volume of literature about Indians in Maryland and Delaware. These publications are not widely known by students and professional scholars. Much of the older literature has become antiquated or obsolete, and many of the standard works are out of print. In Maryland and Delaware a considerable amount of the early literature concerning the aboriginal population was published in the official reports of the Bureau of American Ethnology and the Smithsonian Institution, although some of the most important material appeared in museum reports, university bulletins, and newsletters and journals of local archaeological societies. The most productive of these societies have been the Archaeological Society of Maryland, the Archaeological Society of Delaware, and the Sussex [Delaware] Society for Archeology and History. Before their formation most research depended upon the efforts of conscientious, scientifically minded antiquarians who explored specific topics and investigated single tribes. Work by trained anthropologists and archaeologists was severely lacking.

During the latter part of the nineteenth century,

organized surveys and supervised excavations replaced the haphazard and often destructive practice of amateurs collecting Indian artifacts. The growth of organizational activities, combined with the stimulus given to research by the federal government, clearly influenced archaeological work in the eastern United States. From the outset a major attempt was made to define in historical perspective the salient archaeological manifestations of the Middle Atlantic region. This task was considerably hampered by a paucity of detailed information and by the inability to define cultures that were temporally related and yet spatially separated. The rapid rate of culture change among the eastern Indians after contact with Europeans, the destruction of aboriginal sites by urban and industrial growth, and the blatant pilfering from burial and settlement sites sorely compounded the loss of data.

Such unfavorable circumstances resulted in the East remaining one large, generalized culture area, whereas the West was substantially subdivided because archaeologists found conditions more conducive for the preservation of sites—less urbanization and farming than along the Atlantic seaboard—as well as more complete in ethnohistorical data. Alfred Kroeber confessed he was unable to provide a satisfactory framework for the eastern part of the continent because the culture of this area simply was harder to organize than the rest. Without more detailed information than was then generally available, he concluded that the Atlantic side of North America was relatively uniform in its native culture. W. Fred Kinsey has also noted that the early emphasis on the Adena- and Hopewell-related complexes associated with the Ohio Valley manifestations retarded the recognition of the indigenous culture complexes that occupied areas east of the Appalachian Mountains from the Piedmont Plateau through the Coastal Plain.

In time the East would gain recognition as an area worthy of scholarly investigation. Beginning in the 1930s, research concentrated on archaeological fieldwork and historical study of documentary records. The initial work in Maryland and Delaware by trained archaeologists focused almost exclusively on the reconstruction of the material aspects of prehistoric life, examination of burial customs on the Delmarva peninsula, and location and identification of settlements. In 1933, D. S. Davidson, a member of the Department of Anthropology at the University of Pennsylvania, directed the interests of his students to the Delmarva peninsula. In the same year, through the efforts of H. Geiger Omwake, the Archaeological Society of Delaware was formed. The members of the new organization joined Davidson's students in excavating the Slaughter Creek site in Sussex County, Delaware. The discovery and excavation of several Adena-related burial sites in the Delaware and Chesapeake Bay area spurred further interest in and concern for archaeology. In *Delaware's Buried Past: A Story of Archaeological Adventure* [206], Clinton A. Weslager chronicles the development of archaeological work in the state. Although the necessary information is readily available, no comparable treatment of Maryland exists.

Most of the historical accounts of the aboriginal population of Maryland and Delaware have depended on contemporary published sources. A monumental work of this genre was Raphael Semmes's *Captains and Mariners of Early Maryland* [166], which, relying heavily on the *Archives of Maryland* [123], attempted to narrate the sequence of events following the Indians' contact with European settlers and colonial officials. The meticulous work of Wm. B. Marye in the 1930s and 1940s was a notable exception to this type of research. Utilizing colonial land records housed in the Halls of Records in Annapolis, Maryland, and Dover, Delaware, Marye successfully charted the "Indian Paths of Delmarva Peninsula" [119], located *Indian Towns of the Southeastern Part of Sussex County, Delaware* [122], and identified "Former Indian Sites in Maryland as Located by Early Colonial Records" [118]. Using similar data, Leon de Valinger examined *Indian Land Sales in Delaware* [38], and Weslager elaborated on the same material with "A Discussion of the Family Hunting Territory Question in Delaware" [202].

During the greater part of the nineteenth century little attention was paid to the possibility that small enclaves of Indians remained in the East. Beginning in the 1930s, however, and continuing to the present, a number of scholars—cultural anthropologists, sociologists, geographers, educators, and local antiquarians—directed their research to several population groups of presumed triracial descent. Variously termed mulattoes, mestizos, mixed-bloods, and triracial isolates, the consensus was that they were a people of intermingled Indian, Caucasian, and Negro ancestry. Although the myth of the vanishing Indian in the East had been laid to rest, this new direction of research would create new problems. Brewton Berry, in *Almost White: A Study of Certain Racial Hybrids in the Eastern United States* [12], surveyed these isolated communities and confirmed the general confusion among the White and Black populations as to the origin and social status of these people. In the 1940s, Clinton A. Weslager, Thomas J. Harte, and William H. Gilbert investigated the remnant population of Nanticokes and Piscataways in Maryland and Delaware, but their work emphasized too strongly the issue of race mixture. The most important question to consider is not whether or to what extent these groups are genetically Indian. Rather, the emphasis should be on the process of acculturation, reconstruction of tribal histories, economic and social integration into American society, and the problems of maintaining community and individual identity.

After compiling more than two thousand citations, it has become apparent to me that Maryland and Delaware have had a rich and significant heritage of archaeological exploration and historical investigation. Until very recently the work of these dedicated and unheralded individuals has not achieved widespread notice. In fact, there continues to be a reluctance to acknowledge the wealth of information, both documentary and archaeological, available for understanding the aboriginal, as well as the postcontact period in these states. Approximately forty tribes were present at the time of first contact. The European settlement of Maryland and Delaware resulted in the rapid extinction, amalgamation, acculturation, or removal of many of these tribes. Only through continued careful archaeological research in conjunction with historical investigation will we be able to preserve some understanding of the level of population density through time, the size of family units, bands, and tribes and their concentration and dispersion, the pattern of residence in the villages, subsistence strategies and ecological adjustment to microenvironments, and the numerous nonmaterial facets of the aboriginal culture. This bibliographical essay is the first serious effort to illuminate both the strengths and the weaknesses of the published material pertaining to Indians in Maryland and Delaware, both past and present.

RECOMMENDED WORKS

For the Beginner

[52]   Alice Leczinska L. Ferguson and Henry G. Ferguson, *The Piscataway Indians of Southern Maryland.*

[86]   Robert L. Humphrey and Mary Elizabeth Chambers, *Ancient Washington: American Indian Cultures of the Potomac Valley.*

[143]   Frank W. Porter, III, *A Photographic Survey of Indian River Community.*

[205]   Clinton A. Weslager, *Delaware's Forgotten Folk: The Story of the Moors and Nanticokes.*

[211]   ———, *The Nanticoke Indians: A Refugee Tribal Group of Pennsylvania.*

For a Basic Library Collection

[4]   Edward Arber, ed., *Travels and Works of Captain John Smith, President of Virginia and Admiral of New England, 1580–1631.*

[12]   Brewton Berry, *Almost White: A Study of Certain Racial Hybrids in the Eastern United States.*

[31]   E. A. Dalrymple, ed., *Relatio Itineris in Marylandiam Declaratio Coloniae . . . ad Annum 1638. . . . Narrative of a Voyage to Maryland, by Father Andrew White, S.J. An Account of the Colony of the Lord Baron of Baltimore. Extracts from Different Letters of Missionaries, from the Year 1635 to the Year 1677.*

[44]   Arthur R. Dunlap and Clinton A. Weslager, *Indian Place-Names in Delaware.*

[73]   Clayton C. Hall, ed., *Narratives of Early Maryland, 1633–1684.*

[78]   John G. E. Heckewelder, *History, Manners, and Customs of the Indian Nations Who Once Inhabited Pennsylvania and the Neighboring States.*

[97]   Hamill T. Kenny, *The Origin and Meaning of the Indian Place Names of Maryland.*

[101]   John C. Kraft, ed., "The Pre-European Archaeology of Delaware."

[122] Wm. B. Marye, *Indian Towns of the Southeastern Part of Sussex County, Delaware.*

[166] Raphael Semmes, *Captains and Mariners of Early Maryland.*

[170] Frank G. Speck, "The Naticoke Community of Delaware."

[171] Frank G. Speck, *The Nanticoke and Conoy Indians with a Review of Linguistic Material from Manuscript and Living Sources: An Historical Study.*

[188] Gladys Tantaquidgeon, *A Study of Delaware Indian Medicine Practices and Folk Beliefs.*

[206] Clinton A. Weslager, *Delaware's Buried Past: A Story of Archaeological Adventure.*

[224] Cara L. Wise, *A Handbook for Delmarva Archaeology.*

[227] Henry T. Wright, *An Archaeological Sequence in the Middle Chesapeake Region.*

BIBLIOGRAPHICAL ESSAY

Primary Sources

The principal sources and foundations of any study about Indians in Maryland and Delaware are the printed collections of the *Archives of Maryland* [123], the *Pennsylvania Archives* [139] and *Minutes of the Provincial Council of Pennsylvania* [138], edited by Samuel Hazard, and the *Minutes of House of Assembly of the Government of the Counties of New Castle, Kent and Sussex upon Delaware* [35] and [36]. Many of the proceedings of the delegates and the laws of the Maryland Assembly, not found in the *Archives of Maryland*, are contained in Thomas Bacon's edition of the *Laws of Maryland* [6]. The complete text of all the laws can be found in the *Laws of the State of Maryland* [125] (printed under various titles), which were printed after each session of the assembly. Lawrence Wroth's *A History of Printing in Colonial Maryland* [228] is an authoritative guide to these imprints. *Narratives of Early Maryland* [73], edited by Clayton C. Hall, provides in one convenient volume a collection of significant manuscripts, pamphlets, and contemporary accounts of seventeenth-century Maryland. The *Maryland Historical Magazine* has published various miscellaneous official documents, letters, and diaries interspersed among a great number of articles. The researcher should also be aware of similar printed documents relating to Maryland and Delaware that have been published in the *Pennsylvania Magazine of History* and Biography, *Virginia Magazine of History and Biography, Delaware History,* and the *William and Mary Quarterly.* A neglected source of information about Indian raids, massacres, and treaties were the colonial newspapers, particularly the *Maryland Gazette, Pennsylvania Gazette,* and *Virginia Gazette.*

Bibliographies

There is no comprehensive guide to the published materials of Maryland history. Students seeking bibliographical aid in their research on Indians in Maryland and Delaware should begin with George P. Murdock's *Ethnographic Bibliography of North America* [134], which contains the largest number of references to Maryland and Delaware, although it does not provide thorough coverage of the available literature. Irving Rouse's *An Anthropological Bibliography of the Eastern Seaboard* [154] and the updated edition of it by Alfred K. Guthe and Patricia B. Kelley [72], John O. Brew's *A Selected Bibliography of American Indian Archaeology East of the Rocky Mountains* [17], and Claude E. Schaeffer's and Leo J. Roland's *A Partial Bibliography of the Archaeology of Pennsylvania and Adjacent States* [157] were early efforts to identify the basic literature about the aboriginal population of the Atlantic seaboard. Recently, Roger W. Moeller and John Reid have compiled a fairly comprehensive *Archaeological Bibliography for Eastern North America* [130] that starts from the terminal date (1963) of the Guthe and Kelley bibliography. Because the scope of these bibliographies was so extensive, they merely skimmed the surface of the available published sources. Elizabeth Baer's *Seventeenth Century Maryland: A Bibliography* [7] is an essential reference guide for using the early promotional pamphlets, especially the relations of Maryland [220, 221], published in the seventeenth century, which relate specifically to Maryland.

County and State Histories

State and county histories constitute an important, but often overlooked, source of information about Indians in Maryland and Delaware. The encyclopedic and compendious works of John Thomas Scharf remain a basic reference tool. Scharf's *History of Maryland, from the Earliest Period to the Present Day* [158] chronicles the history of the aboriginal population, the missionary activities of the Jesuits, and the Seven Years War in America. In his *History of Western Maryland* [159] Scharf again devotes chapters to the native Americans, the Seven Years War in America (French and Indian War), and the circumstances surrounding the murder of Logan's family by Michael Cresap. Scharf's *History of Delaware* [160] provides a vivid account of the Indians who inhabited the Eastern Shore of Maryland and discusses in some detail the Lenni-Lenape. George A. Hanson's *Old Kent* [75] briefly discusses the Indians who inhabited Kent Island. Erich Isaac's "Kent Island, Part I: The Period of Settlement" [90], a detailed and informative study, examines William Claiborne's trade activities with the aboriginal population. George Johnston's *History of Cecil County* [94] is an important source on the influence of the Susquehannock and Seneca Indians in Maryland. Elias Jones's *Revised History of Dorchester County, Maryland* [95] devotes a section to Indian history, as does Frederic Emory's *Queen Anne's County, Maryland* [46]. William H. Lowdermilk's *History of Cumberland (Maryland)* [108] is an important and valuable reference to Indians in western Maryland and to the French and Indian War. Horace P. Hobbs's *Pioneers of the Potowmack* [80], though written for a general audience, narrates the European discovery and exploration of the Potomac River and the explorers' numerous encounters with Indians.

The histories of Maryland generally provide a descriptive background of the Indians and their early relations with the European settlers. James McSherry's *History of Maryland* [115], although written in 1849 and revised in 1904, should be consulted. Matthew Page Andrews's *The Founding of Maryland* [3] examines the trouble that developed between the colonists and the Indians. A similar discussion is found in Andrews's *History of Maryland* [2]. A basic reference to the early relations between Calvert's colonists and the Indians is John L. Bozman's *The History of Maryland* [15]. John V. L. McMahon also discusses these early relationships in his *An Historical View of the Government of Maryland*

[113]. Charles B. Clark's *The Eastern Shore of Maryland and Virginia* [22] contains Weslager's brief account, "Indians Tribes of the Eastern Shore of Maryland and Virginia" [212]. Jennings C. Wise's *Ye Kingdome of Accawmacke; or, The Eastern Shore of Virginia in the Seventeenth Century* [225] discusses the Indians residing on the lower portion of the Delmarva peninsula. *Maryland—A History* [201], edited by Richard Walsh and William Lloyd Fox, blatantly ignores the existence of Indians in Maryland.

Archaeology

The years between 1840 and 1914 have been termed the Classificatory-Descriptive period in American archaeology by Gordon R. Willey and Jeremy A. Sabloff. In Maryland and Delaware, archaeology progressed during this period from an emphasis on surface finds and publicizing of private collections to inventory and classification of aboriginal artifacts. There were occasional attempts to discover and identify village sites, but most of the actual excavations at that time were efforts to obtain artifacts, usually the more exotic types of objects, and local controversies still raged concerning the origin and antiquity of the American Indian. During the second half of the nineteenth century the major concern of archaeologists in eastern North America centered specifically on the mounds and their builders in the Ohio and Mississippi valleys and surrounding areas. In 1894, Cyrus Thomas of the Bureau of Ethnology undertook an extensive program of survey and excavation in order to salvage and study the mounds before they were destroyed. Maryland and Delaware did not possess such elaborate earthworks, and in his report on the mounds Thomas noted only the presence of stone graves in Washington County, Maryland.

In isolated cases individuals directed their scientific abilities to the archaeological problems of the Middle Atlantic region. On a local level, Hilborne T. Cresson, Henry C. Mercer, and Elmer R. Reynolds were contributing to the search for knowledge of early pre-Indian man in eastern America, reflecting a debate that continued in the professional and intellectual community. Cresson's *Report upon Pile Structures in Naaman's Creek Near Claymont, Delaware* [27] climaxed nearly three decades of his argument supporting the presence of a pre-Indian man in the Delaware Valley. Henry C. Mercer, curator of the Museum of American and Prehistoric Archaeology at the University of Pennsylvania, questioned the validity of Cresson's evidence. In 1897, Mercer reported his findings in *Researches upon the Antiquity of Man in the Delaware Valley* [129]. Mercer's interpretation was based on his "Exploration of an Indian Ossuary on the Choptank River, Dorchester County, Maryland" [128] and "The Discovery of Aboriginal Remains at a Rock Shelter in Delaware Known as the Indian House" [127]. Elmer R. Reynolds, who had invested considerable time and energy in excavating shell mounds and soapstone quarries in Maryland, summarized his work in "Memoirs on the Pre-Columbian Shell Mounds at Newburg, Maryland and the Aboriginal Shell Mounds of the Potomac and the Wicomico Rivers" [152]. By the close of the century the period of pioneer explorations and speculations was nearing an end. The picture was still very muddled. Several archaeological sites had been discovered and studied, a great quantity of specimens had been collected, and the opportunity had arisen to develop classifications of the artifacts to aid in interpreting this area's culture history.

The emphasis toward classification of archaeological material shifted gradually as archaeologists struggled to make their profession a systematic and scientific discipline. One of the major contributors during this period was William H. Holmes. Holmes, who worked in the United States National Museum and the Bureau of American Ethnology, was specifically interested in prehistoric ceramics and lithic technology. Working with the available literature and inspecting hundreds of pottery collections, in 1903 Holmes published a significant typological and classificatory work, "Aboriginal Pottery of the Eastern United States" [84]. Holmes's monograph identified well-defined pottery regions within the eastern United States and laid a foundation for the analysis of ceramics in North America. Similarly, Thomas Wilson's "Chipped Stone Classification" [223], Gerard Fowke's "Stone Art" [57], William H. Holmes's "Stone Implements of the Potomac-

Chesapeake Tidewater Province" [83], and Warren K. Moorehead's classic two-volume *The Stone Age in North America* [133] were pioneering works in the classification of stone implements. This significant period of classifying prehistoric ceramics and stone implements was followed by a two-decade hiatus of archaeological investigation in Maryland and Delaware. The appearance of organized archaeological activities in the 1930s, however, marked the advent of a new era of research. First, material that had been accumulated during the previous twenty-five years was published. It was apparent that research in Maryland, particularly in the Potomac Valley, had not progressed significantly since Holmes had described and studied most of the major village sites in tidewater Maryland. In fact, D. S. Davidson, discussing the "Problems in the Archaeology of the Delmarva Peninsula" [32], considered the area terra incognita. But this was not to imply that a study of the Delmarva peninsula was without merit. With organized archaeological studies of this region just beginning, Davidson pointed out, it would now be possible to conduct research with reference to the already formulated general problems of eastern North America outlined in the earlier works.

The excavation of sites on the upper Potomac River during the 1940s revealed a greater complexity of cultural areas than indicated by the earlier arbitrary division of the Potomac Valley at the Fall Line. Richard E. Stearns, curator of the Department of Archaeology of the Natural History Society of Maryland, offered a résumé of his archaeological work in tidewater Maryland. "Some Indian Village Sites of Tidewater Maryland" [179] was essentially a comparison of the ceramics and stone artifacts from these sites. Carl Manson's "Marcey Creek Site: An Early Manifestation in the Potomac Valley" [116], Richard G. Slattery's "A Prehistoric Indian Site on Seldon Island, Montgomery County, Maryland" [168], and Richard Stearns's "The Hughes Site: An Aboriginal Village Site on the Potomac River in Montgomery County, Maryland" [178] demonstrated that the important cultural traits of these Piedmont sites included single, flexed burials; triangular arrowpoints; lugged, shell-tempered pottery; and discoidals. Several large sites were also excavated in the lower Potomac River area. One of the most important was the historic Algonkian village of Moyaone. Alice L. L. Ferguson's *Moyaone and the Piscataway Indians* [50] identified the principal cultural traits of the historic Algonkian sites of the lower Potomac as ossuary or group burial, grit-tempered pottery, stemmed projectile points, and stockaded villages. Although research in the 1940s further clarified the boundaries of culture areas and intercultural relationships, technical problems in defining culturally diagnostic artifact complexes persisted. The region's chronology remained very general and, in light of later research, was frequently misinterpreted.

Woodland burial complexes, especially the presence of ossuaries at some sites, attracted considerable attention. D. S. Davidson was concerned with "Burial

Customs in the Delmarva Peninsula and the Question of Their Chronology" [33]. Wm. B. Marye carefully examined "Burial Methods in Maryland and Adjacent States" [120]. Alice Ferguson, who was excavating the Accokeek Site, recorded a "Burial Area in Moyaone" [49] and "An Ossuary Near Piscataway Creek" [51]. In Delaware, Clinton A. Weslager discussed "Ossuaries on the Delmarva Peninsula and Exotic Influences in the Coastal Aspect of the Woodland Pattern" [204]. Although these studies formed the foundation of more recent research on burial customs, chronological and cultural affiliations remained confused and admittedly poorly defined. Undoubtedly among the more intriguing discoveries made in Delaware and Maryland were the implements and ornaments usually associated with the Ohio Valley and New York, such as the Adena and Kipp Island cultures. Ronald A. Thomas has summarized the "Adena Influence in the Middle Atlantic Coast" [189] and discussed the "Webb Phase Mortuary Customs at the Island Field Site" [191]. Ronald A. Thomas and Nancy A. Warren have provided a more detailed account of the Webb Phase component in "A Middle Woodland Cemetery in Central Delaware: Excavations at the Island Field Site" [193].

The establishment of a chronology was one of the most significant obstacles in the development of cultural historical syntheses for regional prehistory. Specifically, the difficulty in placing culture forms in time and space stemmed from the lack of sites showing meaningful stratification and the resulting inability to use geological and paleontological evidence to correlate human or cultural remains with various Holocene levels. In 1952, Karl Schmitt published the first systematic "Archaeological Chronology of the Middle Atlantic States" [161] since the work of Holmes. Borrowing from concepts developed in the Midwest and utilizing the temporal periods of Archaic, Early Woodland, Middle Woodland, and Late Woodland, Schmitt listed components—and in some cases foci—within these periods and described some of their principal traits. In 1955, Clifford Evans's ceramic analysis of Virginia material [47], which included an appendix on projectile points and large blades by C. G. Holland, provided additional chronological information on the Middle Atlantic states. Although general temporal periods had been distinguished for the Middle Atlantic region, research in Delaware and most of the Coastal Plain dealt almost exclusively with Late Woodland material.

The realization that detailed chronological and cultural significance for the Woodland Period could be interpreted from the observed ceramic variability matured slowly. It soon became apparent, however, that ceramics were key elements in identifying external relationships and in constructing regional cultural units. The major turning point in Delaware archaeological studies came in 1948 when the Sussex Society for Archeology and History was organized for the excavation of the Townsend Site, a large Late Woodland manifestation in southern Delaware. By previous arrangement, all the recovered material was analyzed by the Anthropology Department of the Smithsonian Institution. It was not until 1963 that the Sussex Society for Archeology and History issued its report, "The Townsend Site Near Lewes, Delaware" [137]. Earlier, Margaret C. Blaker, who was affiliated with the Smithsonian Institution, had briefly discussed "Pottery Types from the Townsend Site, Lewes, Delaware" [14]. The ceramic typology developed by Blaker, which was published in the Townsend report, paralleled Evans's work on Virginia ceramics. Using a structural approach, where types were defined on the basis of variations in decorative technique and motif and to a lesser extent on form, Blaker defined the Townsend series and its five component types. Unfortunately, neither Blake nor the others who analyzed the Townsend ceramics could establish convincing temporal implications of the typology beyond the general category of Late Woodland.

One of the first productive efforts to establish an absolute temporal framework resulted in 1973 from research on the Western Shore of Maryland. Henry T. Wright's *An Archaeological Sequence in the Middle Chesapeake Region* [227] defined a series of phases and attendant subsistence-settlement patterns. Wright's temporal variation, based on ceramic changes, was only partly successful. Subsequent research by Daniel R. Griffith ("Townsend Ceramics and the Late Woodland of Southern Delaware" [70]) and Wayne E. Clark ("The Application of Regional Research Designs to Contract

Archaeology: The Northwest Transportation Corridor Archaeological Survey Project" [23]) have demonstrated that Wright's Late Woodland sequence is reversed and oversimplified. Daniel R. Griffith and Richard E. Artusy's "A Brief Report on Semisubterranean Dwellings on the Delmarva Peninsula" [71], combining stratigraphic evidence and radiocarbon dates, has firmly placed three of the five types of Blaker's Townsend ceramic typology in a temporal perspective. The Townsend series ranged from A.D. 1000 to contact. Griffith and Artusy's findings indicate a temporal sequence for the Late Woodland with incised Townsend ceramics predating and then continuing concurrently with cord-decorated types until European contact. The work of William M. Gardner and Charles W. McNett in the Potomac Valley in the early 1970s was an integral part of this phase of Maryland and Delaware research to provide a firm chronological footing for future cultural syntheses of at least the Woodland period. "Early Pottery in the Potomac" [59] and "Shell Middens of the Potomac Coastal Plain" [114] laid the foundation for more sophisticated studies in culture history and culture process that are now under way.

Because of the emphasis placed on the study of the Woodland Period in Delaware and Maryland, little effort was made until recently to place artifacts of earlier cultural periods in a firm chronological framework. Beginning in 1965, when the first professional archaeologist to work extensively on the Delmarva peninsula was hired by the state of Delaware, the question of prehistoric man in that area was formally addressed. In 1971, Cara L. Wise compiled *A Handbook for Delmarva Archaeology* [224]. This handbook was designed to meet the needs of both the beginning collector and the professional. Soon after, Ronald A. Thomas prepared "A Brief Survey of Prehistoric Man on the Delmarva Peninsula" [190]. At present, most of the research in Maryland and Delaware is concerned with broad cultural syntheses developed from firmer space/time control of the Woodland Period, while primary research continues to establish a regional chronology for earlier periods.

Culture Area

In an attempt to define culture areas within North America, individual anthropologists have delineated specific areas and designated their cultural affinity based on climate, vegetation, physiography, and culture traits. The classification of North America into culture areas, however, has presented several problems. W. C. McKern's "A Cultural Perspective of Northeastern Area Archaeology" [109], although referring specifically to the Woodland pattern for northeastern North America, raises critical questions in regard to the concept and usefulness of a culture area. The factors of cultural development, movement in time, and cultural diversity reduce the concept of a culture area "to a fleeting picture which cannot be defined

in terms of space and time; and if defined in terms of
space alone, can have no permanency or lasting importance" [109, p. 34]. Cultural groups who occupied
specific geographic areas are better depicted and
analyzed from the perspective of cultural conflict,
change, and complexity than from that of cultural
unity. McKern's alternative to the culture area concept
was to choose an area purely as a geographic division,
arbitrarily selected to limit the subject. Cultural processes and patterns within this area could be examined
as they related to both tradition and environment,
without the false assumption of environmental possession or determinism. James B. Griffin's "Cultural
Changes and Continuity in Eastern United States Archaeology" [68] proposed that successive cultural stages
throughout the eastern United States could be erected
on the basis of local stratigraphy, interchange of specific cultural items, and common possession of definite
cultural concepts at specific chronological periods.
William A. Ritchie, however, in his "Archaeological
Manifestations and Relative Chronology in the Northeast" [153], cautioned that the salient archaeological
manifestations of the Middle Atlantic region were
hampered by the rapid rate of acculturation following
European contact and the destruction of aboriginal
settlement sites by urban and industrial expansion. The
result was a paucity of detailed information with con-
sequent lack of the means to interrelate accurately and
correlate chronologically cultures that were spatially
separated.

One of the most difficult problems in the formation of culture areas has been the question of boundaries. This has proved particularly perplexing in the efforts to study the aboriginal population of Maryland for two reasons. Most of the initial attempts to establish culture areas for North America began with a continental scale of analysis. Inevitably, Indians residing in Maryland and Delaware were placed within the context of a large, ill-defined geographic area frequently referred to as the *East*. Even within a more confined regional approach, Maryland has suffered. Because the colony of Virginia was established and settled first, and the territory that later became Maryland was included in the charter to the Virginia colony, most of the early investigations of the aboriginal population of Maryland were subsumed within studies of Virginia and the Powhatan Confederacy. Furthermore, the establishment of colonial boundaries simply reflected the political expression of arbitrary agreements that resulted in the artificial separation of tribes, placing them under the jurisdiction of specific colonies. Finally, Maryland has been confronted with the geographic problem of being divided by Chesapeake Bay into the Western Shore and the Eastern Shore, with Virginia claiming the lower peninsula as part of her domain. In colonial times Pennsylvania assumed control of the Lower Counties fronting Delaware Bay and the Atlantic Ocean. Within this area resided several distinct tribal groups.

One of the first attempts to classify the aboriginal population of North America was John Wesley Powell's

Indian Linguistic Families of America, North of Mexico [147], which was based principally on word lists. A more recent classification of North American Indian languages is that of Voegelin and Voegelin [198], which distinguished three levels: phylum, family, and language. In each case the aboriginal peoples of Maryland and Delaware were placed in the Algonquian language family. William H. Holmes's "Areas of American Culture Classification Tentatively Outlined as an Aid in the Study of Antiquities" [85], another early attempt to define culture areas of North America, placed Maryland within the North Atlantic area, which extended from Newfoundland and the Saint Lawrence Valley in the north to Georgia in the south. Holmes identified several general characteristics of this culture area. Subsistence in this area was based on hunting and fishing, with agriculture successfully practiced in many of the fertile valleys. The use of stone in building was virtually unknown; dwellings usually were constructed of bark and mats. Stockades were relied upon for village defense. Burial mounds and other earthworks were rare or insignificant in size; and the methods of burial were primitive and varied considerably, with graves yielding simple artifacts used by the people. The use of red iron oxides was a common practice in the burials. In some instances caves and rock shelters were occupied for dwellings and used as burial sites. Holmes considered the ceramic art in a rudimentary stage. The vessels were round-bodied—often conical beneath—decorated with incised lines forming simple geometric figures, with fabric or cord impressions and often, among the Iroquois, with crude figures in relief. Soapstone was used for cooking utensils, tobacco pipes, and ornaments. The spear was not in general use at the time of European contact; the bow and arrow, tomahawk, and club were the principal weapons.

Little more was said or proposed until Clark Wissler argued for the classification of social groups according to their culture traits. Under this classification, based on historical culture data, Maryland was included in the Southeastern area. Kroeber, in his *Cultural and Natural Areas of Native North America* [102], grouped everything east of the Rocky Mountains into the "East," although he did distinguish the Middle Atlantic Slope area, which included the Nanticokes and Piscataways of Maryland. Continuing this macrodesignation of "eastern" or "southeastern" culture areas is Harold E. Driver's *Indians of North America* [41].

Peter P. Cooper, in "The Southeastern Archaeological Area Re-defined" [25], has strongly criticized this aggregating of culture areas in the East because it encompasses too much, makes archaeological interpretations confusing and unwieldy, obscures important distinctions, and fails to shed light on a little-known area. Cooper suggests that a reasonable definition of the Southeast should refer to Virginia, North Carolina, South Carolina, central and eastern Maryland, southern Delaware, eastern West Virginia, and northeastern Georgia. Karl Schmitt [161] narrowed the focus by defining the "Middle Atlantic" as Virginia, Maryland,

Pennsylvania, New Jersey, and Delaware. Clifford Evans's *A Ceramic Study of Virginia Archeology* [47] was a pioneering effort to clarify and delimit the cultural development within the area that Holmes set forth as a single culture province. Following this lead, Robert L. Stephenson assiduously examined the pottery from the Accokeek Creek site and defined a Middle Atlantic Seaboard culture province [181] and [182]. Stephenson affixed rather specific boundaries to this province, according to which the province was bounded by the Rappahannock River on the south and the foothills of the Blue Ridge Mountains on the west. The northern boundary extended along the foothills from Harrisburg, Pennsylvania to the Palisades of the Hudson River. These proposals and interpretations have not gone unnoticed. Louis A. Brennan has offered "A Futher Definition of Stephenson's Middle Atlantic Seaboard Culture Province" [16]. Brennan, comparing materials between the Accokeek Creek site and sites on the lower Hudson, demonstrates a correspondence dating from the entrance into the Atlantic Seaboard culture province of the Taconic tradition of making stemmed points on arrowheads. The character of the entire province changed with the influx of the Taconic people, and the province began its cultural existence at this time. W. Fred Kinsey [100] suggests that the "Middle Atlantic culture province" concept has its greatest utility in the study of Late Archaic cultures.

Tribes

In June, 1608, Captain John Smith and fourteen companions departed from Jamestown to explore the shores of Chesapeake Bay. Smith recorded his encounters at various Indian villages during his voyage. The *Travels and Works of Captain John Smith* [4], edited by Edward Arber, is an indispensable source regarding these early explorations and observations of Chesapeake Bay and its inhabitants. There were several Indian tribes living on the Eastern Shore and other parts of the Delmarva peninsula that Smith did not visit.

Albert Gallatin's *A Synopsis of the Indian Tribes within the United States* [58] was an early and serious effort to accumulate and preserve important data about the remaining tribes in the United States north of Mexico. Considerable information about the Nanticokes and Piscataways and their relationship with the Susquehannocks is provided there. Henry R. Schoolcraft's *History of the Indian Tribes of the United States* [162] briefly sketches the Indian tribes of Maryland. James E. Hancock's "The Indians of the Chesapeake Bay Section" [74], James Mooney's "Indian Tribes of the District of Columbia" [131], and Clinton A. Weslager's "Indian Tribes of the Delmarva Peninsula" [203], "Indian Tribes of the Eastern Shore of Maryland and Virginia" [212], and "The Anthropological Position of the Indian Tribes of the Delmarva Peninsula" [209] are important attempts to identify and locate the various tribes that resided in Maryland and Delaware and to correct many of the errors and misconceptions that had permeated the literature. Bernard G. Hoffman's "Ancient Tribes Revisited" [82] presents a more recent analysis of the basic features of American Indian tribal distribution and movement in the northeastern United States during the colonial period through available contemporary historical sources. Two succinct sources on individual tribes in Maryland and Delaware are Frederick W. Hodge's two-volume *Handbook of American Indians North of Mexico* [81], soon to be complimented by the forthcoming Smithsonian Institution volume on the Southeast in the *Handbook of North American Indians* [56], and John R. Swanton's *The Indian Tribes of North America* [187].

Nanticokes

The identification of the Nanticokes has been somewhat obscured by the generic application of the term to all tribes residing on the Eastern Shore of Maryland and by their presumed affiliation with the Delaware Indians. John G. E. Heckewelder, in his *History, Manners and Customs of the Indian Nations* [78], stated that the Nanticokes referred to themselves as Nentego, a variant of the Delaware Unechtgo or Unalachtigo, meaning tidewater people. Clinton A. Weslager has clarified this confusion by demonstrating that the Unalachtigo were not the Nanticokes known to modern Delawares as the Winetok. Furthermore, the colonial authorities of Maryland readily distinguished as separate entities the Nanticokes, Choptanks, Assateagues, and other tribes [218] and [207]. The Nanticokes proper occupied the territory forming the drainage system of the Nanticoke River.

Clinton A. Weslager's *Delaware's Forgotten Folk: The Story of the Moors and Nanticokes* [205] remains a standard reference on the general history of the Nanticokes but emphasizes too strongly the issue of miscegenation in their ancestry. Weslager's *The Nanticoke Indians: A Refugee Tribal Group of Pennsylvania* [211] narrates their migration from the Eastern Shore of Maryland to Canada. Frank G. Speck's *The Nanticoke and Conoy Indians* [171], while providing a review of linguistic material from manuscript and living sources, also portrays the social position of the Nanticokes among the Six Nations on the Grand River Reservation in Canada. Speck's "The Nanticoke Community of Delaware" [170], which provides ethnographic data about the Nanticokes who chose to remain in Maryland, is essential reading for an understanding of their acculturation during the early years of the twentieth century. Frank W. Porter's "A Century of Accommodation: The Nanticokes in Colonial Maryland" [145] details their continuous effort to cope successfully with the permanent presence of European settlers. Christian Feest's "The Nanticokes and Neighboring Tribes [48], in volume 15 of the new *Handbook of North American Indians* [195], is a succinct summary.

Piscataways

The Piscataways, also known as the Conoys, belonged to the Algonquian linguistic family and, according to their own account, were related to the Nanticokes. Their principal village, called Moyaone, was on the Potomac River below the mouth of Piscataway Creek. The history of the Piscataways in many ways parallels that of the Nanticokes. Severely reduced in number, they were assigned a tract of land on an island in the Potomac River. The Susquehannock Indians attacked the Piscataways in 1675, eventually driving them to Conojoholo in Pennsylvania, where they joined with the Nanticokes. Wm. B. Marye's "Piscattaway" [117], relying predominantly on material obtained from the *Archives of Maryland* [123] and other early documents, authoritatively reconstructs the history of this tribe. William C. MacLeod examines the kinship system of the Piscataways in his "Piscataway Royalty: A Study in Stone Age Government and Inheritance Rulings" [111].

In 1935, Alice L. L. Ferguson and Henry G. Ferguson began the excavation of an Indian village site along the edge of the Potomac River, which they tentatively identified as Moyaone. Alice Ferguson published her initial findings in *Moyaone and the Piscataway Indians* [50], which was later revised as *The Piscataway Indians of Southern Maryland* [52]. After Mrs. Ferguson's death in 1951, Robert L. Stephenson was assigned to restudy the ceramics and other artifacts. Stephenson's *The Ac-*

cokeek Creek Site [183], which incorporated much of the Ferguson material, establishes the historical setting of the Piscataways, discusses the excavations and fieldwork, and analyzes the enormous collection of artifacts obtained from the site. Stephenson also presented his findings in *The Prehistoric People of Accokeek Creek* [181]. A general survey of the Piscataways is provided by Robert L. Humphrey and Mary E. Chambers's *Ancient Washington: American Indian Cultures of the Potomac Valley* [86]. William H. Gilbert discusses "The Wesorts of Southern Maryland: An Outcasted Group" [61], a large population claiming descent from the Piscataway Indians.

Susquehannocks

Although the Susquehannock Indians resided along the Susquehanna River in southeastern Pennsylvania, during the seventeenth century they played a vital role in the development of Indian-White relations in Maryland. War between the Susquehannocks and the colony of Maryland broke out in 1642. The Piscataways, secured as allies by Maryland authorities, afforded protection to the settlers by acting as a buffer between them and the Susquehannocks. Eventually, both the Piscataways and the Susquehannocks suffered a serious decline in population because of the incessant warfare. In the seventeenth century George A. Alsop, an indentured servant in Maryland, wrote *A Character*

of the Province of Maryland [1], which remains a unique
account of the Susquehannock, describing them as a
well-disposed people living under a well-ordered government. Donald A. Cadzow's "Archaeological Studies
of the Susquehannock Indians of Pennsylvania" [20]
presents a reasonably complete account of this tribe,
based on historical records and archaeological material.
*A Brief Description of Indian Life and Indian Trade of the
Susquehannock Indians* [103], by David H. Landis, is in-
teresting from the perspective of early European-
Indian trade, a theme that has been substantially
elaborated on in Francis Jennings's study "The Indian
Trade of the Susquehanna Valley" [91]. William A.
Hunter has also emphasized "The Historic Role of the
Susquehannocks" [87] because of their residence on
the lower Susquehanna River and their trade relations
with the Iroquois and the colony of Maryland. Placing
the subject in the context of shifting relations of power
and dependency among specific Indian tribes and
specific European colonies, Jennings's provocative
essay "Glory, Death and Transfiguration: The
Susquehannock Indians in the Seventeenth Century"
[92] has clarified many of the traditional interpretations of the Susquehannocks.

Choptanks

The Choptank Indians have often been mistakenly
regarded as a subgroup of the Nanticokes or as
synonymous with the Nanticokes. Clinton A. Weslager's

"Wynicaco—A Choptank Chief" [207] briefly discusses their history and the succession of descent among the Choptanks, demonstrating that they were clearly distinct from the Nanticokes. Jane Henry's "The Choptank Indians of Maryland under the Proprietary Government" [79] investigates the failure of the Maryland authorities to maintain a successful relationship with the Choptanks because they did not preserve their land base.

Other Tribes

Although the Delaware Indians, who occupied the valley of the Delaware River and certain adjacent areas, were influential in the early contacts with Europeans, the fur trade in the middle colonies, and initial settlement of the northeastern part of the Delmarva peninsula, no attempt is made here to discuss this tribe. Clinton A. Weslager's *The Delaware Indians: A History* [216] and *The Delawares: A Critical Bibliography* [219] provide detailed coverage of this significant tribe. Other less-known tribes have been treated briefly in Sarah Clayton's "The Potomac (Patawomeke) Indians" [24], William J. Graham's *The Indians of Port Tobacco River, Maryland, and Their Burial Places* [66], Wm. B. Marye's "The Wiccomiss Indians of Maryland" [121], and Clinton A. Weslager's *The Accomac and Accohannock Indians from Early Relations* [214].

Subsistence Strategies

The subsistence strategies of the Nanticokes and other Algonkian tribes reflected an economic adjustment to differing ecological zones. Ronald A. Thomas et al., analyzing "Environmental Adaptation on Delaware's Coastal Plain" [192], identify six microenvironments: (1) poorly drained woodlands, (2) transitional woodlands, (3) well-drained woodlands, (4) tidal marshes and estuaries, (5) permanent bodies of fresh water, and (6) saltwater bays and oceans. Determining the flora and fauna used as food and their seasonal fluctuations, and using archaeological data, Griffith, in his "Ecological Studies of Prehistory" [69], postulated four possible types of human settlement patterns to exploit these ecological niches: seasonal camps, permanent camps, semipermanent camps, and transient camps. Early visitors to the environs of Chesapeake Bay noted this seasonal migration of the aboriginal population to food resources. Sir Richard Greeneville, who visited Virginia from 1585 to 1586, stated that "the Savages disband into small groups and disperse to different places to live upon shell fish. Other places afford fishing and hunting while their fields are being prepared for the planting of corn" [67, p. 338]. Captain John Smith vividly portrayed this seasonal subsistence strategy [4, p. 68]: "In March and April they live much upon their fishing, weares; and feed on fish, Turkies and Squirrels. In May and June they plant their fieldes; and live most of Acornes, walnuts, and fish. But to mend their diet, some disperse themselves in small companies, and live upon fish, beasts, crabs, oysters, land Torteyses, strawberries, mulberries, and such like. In June, Julie, and August, they feed upon the roots of Tocknough, berries, fish and green wheat."

Later research has clarified and expanded our knowledge of the Indians' subsistence strategies. In *An Analysis of Coastal Algonquian Culture* [54], Regina Flannery argued that agriculture and fishing were important in Maryland but that there was considerable emphasis on hunting as well. Although maize, beans, and squash were the primary horticultural products, the planting of watermelons was also observed by the members of a "Voyage to Maryland, 1705–1706" [135]. Gretchen Beardsley has demonstrated the importance of "The Groundnut as Used by the Indians of Eastern North America" [8]. Various individuals observed the use of the wooden digging stick among the Indians along the Potomac River, probably the Piscataways; and archaeological evidence confirms the use of bone, shell, and stone hoes. Weslager has directed attention to "The Non-food Use of Corn in the Domestic Economy of the Eastern Indians" [210].

The most common and widely observed hunting technique employed by the Algonkian Indians in Maryland involved rousing the game by setting fire to the brush and driving the animals into traps. Hu Maxwell's "The Use and Abuse of Forests by the Virginia Indians" [126] considers the ecological effect of fire as a hunting technique. The Indians were also extremely adept at using various types of snares and traps. Many of these methods of hunting still persist among the Nanticokes. During his ethnographic investigations of "The Nanticoke Community of Delaware" [170], Speck recorded the use of the box trap made from a hollowed gum log and several choking or spring snares. Chesapeake Bay and its many tributaries offered a rich resource of marine life. The Indians of Maryland and Delaware had devised rather ingenious methods of exploiting these food sources. A. Crozier, in "Fishing Methods of the Indians of the Delmarva Region" [28], noted the emphasis on seines, set lines, and weirs. In an early monograph, Francis Jordan called attention to *Aboriginal Fishing Stations on the Coast of the Middle Atlantic States* [96] and stressed their significance for those studying the domestic economy of these aboriginal fishermen and their means of subsistence. Through the use of "Photoarchaeological Analysis of Potomac River Fish Traps" [186], Carl H. Strandberg and Ray Tomlinson have recorded the location of "Ancient Indian Fishtraps in the Potomac River" [185]. In a manner similar to his study of surviving Nanticoke hunting techniques, Speck collected considerable data on devices for taking fish and other marine life. Eel-pots, netting needles, mesh sticks, measuring blocks for making nets, and fykes were still being used by the Nanticokes in the early 1900s.

Material Culture and Technology

The most numerous prehistoric artifacts that have survived are made of stone. Our understanding of the prehistory of Maryland and Delaware is based in part on the analysis of these artifacts. In *A Handbook for Delmarva Archaeology* [224], Cara L. Wise provides a detailed outline and discussion of stone artifacts associated with the Delmarva peninsula. Elwood S. Wilkins has recently discussed "The Lithics of the Delaware and Nanticoke Indians" [222], and M. James Blackman has published "The Geochemical Analysis of Jasper Artifacts and Source Material from Delaware and Pennsylvania" [13]. In the late nineteenth century Elmer R. Reynolds explored several "Aboriginal Soapstone Quarries in the District of Columbia" [151]. David I. Bushnell examined "The Use of Soapstone by the Indians of the Eastern United States" [19]. Recently, Henry H. Hutchinson and David Marine have offered "Further Information Re. Soapstone Bowls, Quarries and Artifacts" [89].

The Nanticoke Indians, who resided on the Eastern Shore, were renowned for their powers of sorcery and their ability to derive "poisons" from local flora. Gladys Tantaquidgeon, in *A Study of Delaware Indian Medicine Practices and Folk Beliefs* [188], included a section on Nanticoke medical practices. Clinton A. Weslager's *Magic Medicines of the Indians* [217] contains a chapter on "Nanticoke and 'Moor' Medicine." Frank

G. Speck's "The Nanticoke Community of Delaware" [170] also lists various herbal cures and folk remedies, as does Weslager's *Delaware's Forgotten Folk* [205]. Speck's "A Maker of Eel-Pots among the Nanticokes of Delaware" [177] contains information on the art of basketry, a skill thought to have become obsolete. Speck's *Gourds of the Southeastern Indians* [172] considers the domestic use of gourds.

Language

It has been generally accepted that the Nanticokes on the Eastern Shore and the Piscataways on the Western Shore spoke a common language. Most of our linguistic data for these tribes are based on brief vocabularies compiled in the eighteenth and nineteenth centuries. Ives Goddard's "Eastern Algonquian Languages" [65] reviews what is known of the language of the Nanticokes and Piscataways and stresses the scantiness of the sources that are available. James C. Pilling's *Bibliography of the Algonquian Languages* [142] lists the known published works containing Nanticoke and Piscataway vocabularies. Because many of these vocabularies were obtained from remnant groups of Indians, they may reflect the language of any of the local groups that together formed a composite tribe. Arthur R. Dunlap's "A Bibliographical Discussion of the Indian Languages of the Delmarva Peninsula" [42] examines the scope and relative value of the records and studies of the Nanticoke and Lenape vocabularies. Much to the dismay of modern Algonquian linguists, Father Andrew White's grammar, dictionary, and catechism written in the language of the Maryland Indians has been lost in the library of the Vatican. One of the more productive avenues of linguistic research in Maryland and Delaware has been the study of Indian place-names. The Indian place-names of Maryland and Delaware have long been disassociated from any living Algonquian language. In many instances the place-names—thoroughly Anglicized—have survived only as proper nouns on contemporary maps and in the current English vocabulary. Most of our knowledge of early Indian place-names is based upon the records made by Europeans. These records are unsatisfactory because they are incomplete; Europeans had difficulty in transcribing exactly what they heard; and the names that were first recorded were often copied inaccurately by later writers. Charles W. Bump's "Indian Place-Names in Maryland" [18] was an early attempt to study this problem. Relying on comparative linguistic studies, Hamill T. Kenny has recently investigated *The Origin and Meaning of the Indian Place Names of Maryland* [97]. Arthur R. Dunlap and Clinton A. Weslager used similar methods in their study, *Indian Place-Names in Delaware* [44].

Population and Demography

How many Native Americans were present in the Middle Atlantic region when the first Europeans arrived at the beginning of the sixteenth century? A review of the published literature dealing with the controversial issues of prehistoric population size, demographic pattern, and carrying capacity of this area reveals a significant disparity in population estimates. Population figures for aboriginal Maryland and Delaware have been derived from two levels of analysis: tribe-by-tribe inventories and hemispheric estimates.

James Mooney was the first modern scholar to offer a tribe-by-tribe estimate for America north of Mexico. In 1910 Mooney published his initial estimate of the aboriginal population at the time of European contact in the *Handbook of American Indians North of Mexico* [81]. Although Mooney had contemplated a book-length work, he died before completing the project. John R. Swanton discovered that Mooney had complete aboriginal estimates for all tribal groups and had written a summary discussion for each of fifteen identified tribal areas. In 1928 Mooney's *The Aboriginal Population of America North of Mexico* [132] was posthumously edited and published by Swanton. Douglas H. Ubelaker has examined "The Sources and Methodology for Mooney's Estimates of North American Indian Population" [197] and concludes that the totals in Mooney's manuscript notes at the Smithsonian Institution are higher for many tribes than those in his published list.

Most of the recent estimates of aboriginal population have used Mooney's work as a point of departure. William C. MacLeod, in *The American Indian Frontier* [112], expressed some dissatisfaction with Mooney's estimates and produced consistently higher figures for the density of the native population of Maryland, Delaware, and Virginia, although he used virtually the same sources as Mooney. In 1939 Alfred L. Kroeber, in *Cultural and Natural Areas of Native North America* [102], reviewed Mooney's tribal estimates, adjusted them on the basis of his own work, substantially reduced the figures for California, and calculated and mapped culture-area densities. John R. Swanton, in his state-by-state summary *The Indian Tribes of North America* [187], continued this pattern of compiling tribal population estimates with minimal analysis. Henry F. Dobyn's "Estimating Aboriginal American Population: An Appraisal of Techniques with a New Hemispheric Estimate" [39] calculated aboriginal population size by considering the rate at which population numbers were being diminished as a consequence of European contact. Dobyns examined the rate of depopulation in different areas of the western hemisphere and produced a standard depopulation ratio of twenty to one. Following the logic of this ratio, he estimated precontact Indian populations ten times larger than the estimates of Mooney and Kroeber. For a comprehensive review of the various theories and methods employed to estimate

the aboriginal population, Denevan's edited work, *The
Native Population of the Americas in 1492* [37], and
Dobyn's *Native American Historical Demography: A Critical
Bibliography* [40] should be consulted.
Until recently, detailed research specifically on
population and demography has been conspicuously
lacking in the Middle Atlantic region. The earliest
population figures for Maryland and Delaware are derived from the observations of Captain John Smith.
Aside from scattered attempts to determine the
number of Indians remaining in Maryland and Delaware during the eighteenth century, no major effort
was made to determine the demographic characteristics
of the aboriginal population until the twentieth century. Raphael Semmes's "Aboriginal Maryland, 1608–
1689" [165], relying on the writings of John Smith, was
the first attempt to estimate the total population of
Maryland. Smith had generally referred to an Indian
village as containing so many men or warriors, calculat-
ing the proportion of fighting men to the rest of the
Indian population as approximately one warrior out of
each three inhabitants. Semmes offered a conservative
estimate of about 6,500 Indian inhabitants for early
seventeenth century Maryland. Reamor R. DeLaBarre's
unpublished master's thesis, "Chesapeake Bay Indian
Population" [34], reviews both ethnohistorical sources
of the seventeenth century and recent population estimates and concludes that there was a greater population density in this area in 1600 than previous studies
had suggested. In 1971 Douglas H. Ubelaker, in his

"Reconstruction of Demographic Profiles from Ossuary Skeletal Samples: A Case Study from the Tidewater Potomac" [196], found skeletal and documentary evidence that the Piscataways—a group Mooney estimated at 2,000—actually numbered from 7,200 to 8,400. Furthermore, this total suggests a population density of 1.2 persons per square kilometer, half again as much as MacLeod's estimate for tidewater Virginia.

It should be obvious from the above discussion that whether we employ ethnohistorical sources, archaeological evidence, or the techniques of physical anthropology, precise population figures and demographic characteristics for the Middle Atlantic region will remain a controversial area of investigation. The absence of sufficient ethnohistorical data, the lack of adequate skeletal samples, and the biased nature of theoretical demographic studies make it difficult to arrive at estimates of total population size.

Early Voyages, Explorations, and Descriptions

David B. Quinn, one of the most renowned authorities on the voyages and explorations to North America, has written a detailed account entitled *North America from Earliest Discovery to First Settlements: The Norse Voyages to 1612* [150]. Quinn has also edited a collection of documents relating to European contact with North America between about A.D. 1000 and A.D. 1600 [149]. The vividly illustrated texts of *The Discovery of*

North America [30], edited by William P. Cumming, Raleigh A. Skelton, and David B. Quinn, and its companion volume, *The Exploration of North America* [29], are invaluable reference sources. Bernard C. Steiner, in his *Descriptions of Maryland* [180], has compiled a chronological bibliography of specific references to Maryland found in the written accounts of early explorers, seventeenth-century guidebooks and propaganda pamphlets, travel accounts, and works of fiction.

The circumstances surrounding many of the early voyages along the Atlantic coast of North America, particularly those of voyagers entering the waters of Chesapeake Bay, are shrouded in mystery, and the reputed contacts with aborigines are equally dubious. We cannot discount, however, the strong possibility that some of these voyagers did explore the coastline and establish contact with the inhabitants. Harry F. Covington, in "The Discovery of Maryland; or, Verrazano's Visit to the Eastern Shore" [26], argues convincingly that in 1524 Giovanni da Verrazano sailed along the coast from the Carolinas to Maine, actually exploring the Eastern Shore of Maryland, which he referred to as Arcadia. In addition to encountering several of the inhabitants, Verrazano and his men kidnapped a young Indian boy and frightened his companions by firing a salvo over their heads. Lawrence C. Wroth's *The Voyages of Giovanni da Verrazano* [229], a thoroughly researched and documented account of Verrazano's expedition between 1524–28, confirms the voyager's early visit to Maryland. Louis D. Scisco documented the Spanish claim for the early "Discovery of the Chesapeake Bay" [163] and has examined the "Voyage of Vincente Gonzalez in 1588" [164], during which Gonzalez sailed along the shore of Chesapeake Bay but apparently did not communicate with the Indians.

Even after its discovery, the actual extent of Chesapeake Bay was not known until John Smith made a tour of its waters. The *Travels and Works of Captain John Smith* [4] contains the publications resulting from Smith's explorations in the New World and is invaluable to an understanding of the initial descriptions of Maryland and its inhabitants. A less-known, but certainly important, voyage was the brief journey made by Cyprian Thorowgood in April and May of 1634 at the request of Father Andrew White for the purpose of establishing trade relations with the Susquehannock Indians. George E. Gifford and Marion Tingling have discussed the identity of Thorowgood and transcribed the text of his journey in "A Relation of a Voyage to the Head of the Bay" [60]. Two excellent and revealing accounts of the Indians of Maryland before their intensive contact with Europeans are Henry Fleet's "A Brief Journal of a Voyage Made in the Bark 'Warwick' to Virginia and Other Parts of the Continent of America" [55] and Colonel Henry Norwood's "A Voyage to Virginia" [136]. In 1621, Henry Fleet was captured by the Anacostan Indians and remained among them for several years, learning their language and customs. By 1627, Fleet had returned to England, inducing William Cloberry, a London merchant, to finance a vessel with which he could traffic with the Indians. Returning to the Indian town of Yowaccomoco (later St. Mary's City), Fleet resumed his residence among the Indians and traded extensively with them for furs. Upon the arrival of Governor Leonard Calvert, Fleet acted as interpreter during Calvert's negotiations with the Indians. Henry Norwood, a relative of Governor William Berkeley of Virginia, planned to seek his fortune in Virginia. After a rather dismal voyage on the *Virginia Merchant,* during which he was forced to purchase rats for food, Norwood and several passengers were abandoned on Fenwick's Island by a mutinous crew. Wandering through the lower peninsula of the Eastern Shore, Norwood and his companions lived with several of the Indian tribes.

Missionaries and Their Missions

Jesuit missions were introduced in Maryland at an early date. Clifford M. Lewis and Albert J. Loomie's *The Spanish Jesuit Mission in Virginia, 1570–1572* [106] supports, through the use of historical and archaeological evidence, the contention that Spanish Jesuits had established a mission among the Indians living along Chesapeake Bay. The most detailed and authoritative source concerning the Jesuit missionaries who accompanied Lord Baltimore's colonists is Father Andrew

White's "Relatio Itineris in Marylandiam" [31] edited by E. A. Dalrymple. Father Andrew White, whom Joseph A. Le May calls the "apostle of Maryland" [105], was a linguist, explorer, priest, theologian, anthropologist, and writer. Le May has diligently researched the rare manuscripts and publications attributed to Father White and concludes that he not only wrote part or all of the four earliest colonization tracts about Maryland, but recorded some of the earliest explorations in Maryland and encounters with the Indians. Richard H. Tierney has focused specifically on him in "Father Andrew White, S.J., and the Indians" [194].

Lord Baltimore, in an early promotional tract, publicly declared that his purpose in colonizing Maryland was "not to think so much of Planting fruits and trees in a land so fruitful, as of sowing the seeds of Religion and piety." By June of 1639, the Jesuit missionaries had dispersed and established missions among several of the tribes. B. U. Campbell's "Early Missions among the Indians in Maryland" [21] details the Jesuits' efforts to proselytize the Indians. Shedding light on this important period are the *Extracts from Different Letters of Missionaries, from the Year 1635 to the Year 1677* that E. A. Dalrymple appended to his translation of Father White's *Relatio Itineris in Marylandiam* [31]. Edwin W. Beitzell, relying on primary historical sources, discusses *The Jesuit Missions of St. Mary's County, Maryland* [10]. John G. Shea's *History of the Catholic Missions among the Indian Tribes of the United States* [167] devotes some attention to the "Maryland Mission."

Despite the apparent success of the Jesuit missionaries in gaining converts, their work did not proceed unhampered. In their attempts to live with the Indians, the Jesuits had secured land directly from them. Such a practice was contrary to proprietary policy. Lord Baltimore disallowed their holdings, forced the Jesuits to relinquish their Indian lands, and expelled them from the colony. However, the close association and daily contact between the missionaries and the various tribes clearly produced changes in both the material and the nonmaterial culture of the Indians. How pervasive these nonmaterial changes were is open to debate. On the one hand, the conversions and baptisms that the missionaries so strongly emphasized were perhaps the Indians' way of accommodating the physical presence of the Jesuits. One must also consider the strong possibility that some of the conversions depicted by the Jesuits were attempts to satisfy their superiors in Europe and the authorities in Maryland as to the success of their activities [145].

Two Moravian missionaries, George H. Loskiel and John G. E. Heckewelder, were particularly important in the efforts to proselytize the Indians in Maryland and Pennsylvania in the eighteenth century. Each wrote a detailed account of his work and tried to preserve whatever information he could about the aboriginal heritage of his converts. Although their work is invaluable to an understanding of the missionary activity of the eighteenth century, Loskiel and Heckewelder accepted uncritically the data their informants gave. Nevertheless, if used with discretion,

Loskiel's *History of the Mission of the United Brethren among the Indians in North America* [107] and Heckewelder's *History, Manners and Customs of the Indian Nations Who Once Inhabited Pennsylvania and the Neighboring States* [78] can be useful sources of information.

Land Tenure and Reservations

A surprisingly neglected topic in the study of Indians in Maryland and Delaware has been aboriginal land tenure, land encroachment by Europeans, and the provision of reservations by colonial authorities. Information derived from early seventeenth century sources indicates that the initial practice of purchasing the land from the Indians established a precedent, at least in theory, for future land transactions. Unfortunately for the Indians, a substantial inconsistency existed between Lord Baltimore's official interpretation of the legal status of Indian land titles and the colonists' voluntary purchase of them. John Kilty's *The Land-holder's Assistant* [99] allocates a short chapter to the subject of Indian lands, in which he highlights the disputes, treaties, and other transactions between proprietary government and the Indians. Charles C. Royce's study, *Indian Land Cessions in the United States* [155], devotes a section to Maryland's policy toward the Indians. In an unpublished master's thesis, Myriam Stottnero-Montero examines "The Rights of the Indians in America and the English Land Policies in the Seventeenth Century Colonies in America" [184].

Jane Henry, focusing on proprietary policy with regard to the property rights of "The Choptank Indians of Maryland under the Proprietary Government" [79], concludes that large-scale encroachment on Indian land vastly exceeded the ability of the proprietor of Maryland to control it. Many ambitious settlers, apparently unable to obtain grants of land directly from the proprietor, puchased land from the Indians and then produced their Indian deeds as proof of title to the land. Exasperated by the loss of their land and fearing further conflict with the White settlers, the Choptanks, and later the Nanticokes, requested the Maryland authorities to provide them with tracts of land legally established by grants from Lord Baltimore. The Maryland Assembly responded with the creation of the Choptank, Chicone, and Broad Creek reservations. Henry H. Hutchinson, relying upon data from the *Archives of Maryland* [123], has reconstructed the boundaries of the "Indian Reservations of the Maryland Provincial Assembly on the Middle Delmarva Peninsula" [88].

Permanent residence on reservations, however, proved antithetical to the seasonal subsistence strategy of the Indians because it restricted their mobility and their access to microenvironments within their habitat during critical seasons of the year. Refusing to emigrate, several Nanticoke families remained in Maryland and adopted what Frank W. Porter terms specific "Strategies for Survival" [146] in order to survive and preserve their Indian identity in the presence of numerically superior Euro-Americans. Porter has suggested that a significant key to understanding the successful survival and persistence of the Nanticokes lies in an analysis of the family hunting territory system. Accustomed to dispersing to remote areas for long periods of isolation, individual Nanticoke families who remained in their hunting territories would have been able to subsist in their traditional habitat even though much of their land had been preempted by European settlers.

In his "Family Hunting Band as the Basis of Algonkian Social Organization" [169], Frank G. Speck defined the family hunting group as a "kinship group composed of folks united by blood or marriage, having the right to hunt, trap, and fish in a certain inherited district bounded by some rivers, lakes, or other natural landmarks." These territories had not only ties of kinship, but a community of land and interest. The long-established practice of small family hunting groups dispersing in the woods promoted family isolation and a permanency of residence in a particular territory. Although a large part of Speck's data was derived from northeastern Algonkian tribes living in the Eastern Sub-Arctic region, he contended, on the assumption that the ethnically related Algonkian inhabiting areas southward into Virginia were similarly organized, that all of the Atlantic coast tribes maintained the same institution. Following the lead of Speck, Anthony F. C. Wallace, in his "Political Organization and Land Tenure among the Northeastern Indians" [200], proposed that among the Delaware and other Algonkian coastal tribes there seems to have been a definite principle of individual or kin ownership in severalty similar to the family hunting ground system of the northern Algonkians. William C. MacLeod [110], utilizing primary sources in the form of land deeds, demonstrated the positive existence of the hereditary family hunting territory as the basis of social organization among the tribes of the Delaware River valley. Leon de Valinger, studying *Indian Land Sales in Delaware* [38], hinted about the presence of the family hunting territory in Delaware when he argued that the Indians exercised authority within the bounds of their "kingdoms." Clinton A. Weslager, reinterpreting de Valinger's data, suggested that these kingdoms were in fact family hunting territories, thus extending the existence of the family hunting territory southward into Kent and Sussex counties in Delaware [202].

Migration

By the end of the seventeenth century only the Nanticokes and Choptanks on the Eastern Shore and a small contingent of Piscataway Indians on the Western Shore had withstood nearly seventy years of mounting pressure and conflict created by continuous contact with the European settlers. While many of the smaller, less-known tribes had been forced to disperse and were later absorbed into other tribes, some groups simply vanished leaving no evidence about their fate. The

Susquehannocks resorted to hostility and war to resist the Marylanders but were eventually forced to migrate to Pennsylvania and New York. The Piscataways allied themselves with the Maryland colonists only to be betrayed. The Nanticokes ultimately abandoned their villages on the Eastern Shore and migrated to Pennsylvania, New York, and Canada. Clinton A. Weslager's *The Nanticoke Indians: A Refugee Tribal Group of Pennsylvania* [211] narrates the migration of the Nanticokes to Canada from their home on the Eastern Shore of Maryland. The *Moravian Journals Relating to Central New York 1745–66* [9] and the [Pennsylvania Archives] *Colonial Records* [140] contain substantial information about the Nanticokes and Piscataways during their temporary residence in New York and Pennsylvania. Harry E. Bender's "The Nanticoke Indians in Lancaster County" [11], David H. Landis's "Conoy Indian Town and Peter Bezaillon" [104], and Barry C. Kent's "Conoy Town on the Lower Susquehanna River" [98] provide further information about specific Nanticoke and Piscataway settlements in Pennsylvania. Charles M. Johnston's *The Valley of the Six Nations: A Collection of Documents on the Indian Lands of the Grand River* [93] illustrates the political and economic plight of the Nanticoke minority among the Iroquois. Frank G. Speck, who visited descendants of the Nanticokes and Piscataways in Canada [171], attempted to unearth ethnographic data that would shed some light on their past. In 1852, a small contingent of Nanticokes from Canada returned to Maryland and claimed five thousand acres of land that they contended had been reserved for them by the Maryland Assembly. In a *Report of the Select Committee on the Claims of the Nanticoke Indians* [124], Maryland officials, after considerable deliberation, concluded that the Nanticokes had legally relinquished all their land.

Strategies for Survival

After the departure of the Nanticokes and Piscataways from Maryland in the 1740s and the final purchase in 1801 of a one-hundred-acre tract of land that had been set aside for a small remnant group of Choptanks, the Indians became a forgotten people. Nevertheless, several families of Indian descent remained in southern Maryland and on the Eastern Shore. In "Strategies for Survival: The Nanticokes in a Hostile World" [146], Frank W. Porter attempts to determine the processes whereby the surviving Nanticokes were integrated into the economic and social institutions of nineteenth-century rural Sussex County, Delaware. One of the most important institutions of White society that the Nanticokes could use to establish and preserve themselves as a community was private property obtained by acquiring legal title to land. This property afforded the Nanticokes a base upon which the Indian River community would later develop. In order to reconstruct the evolving system of land tenure that the survivors of the Nanticoke and Piscataway tribes participated in, the researcher is totally dependent on the data contained in the early land records, wills, inventories of estates, and real and personal property tax lists. Several factors account for the paucity of evidence concerning the land tenure of the Nanticokes. Not only are manuscript sources incomplete, but during the nineteenth century no precise criteria existed for determining the racial status of the Indians. The records include no designation for Indian. Instead, local tax assessors, census takers, and other public officials classified the Indians as being either mulattoes or "colored" people. Furthermore, many land transactions were oral agreements that were never recorded; and, presumably, most of the Indians at this date were illiterate, which explains the absence of private papers. In addition to the land records, the wills and inventories of estates provide some insight on the gradual accumulation of material property by these Indian families.

After the 1831 slave revolt in Virginia led by Nat Turner, Whites throughout the South made every effort to keep Blacks apart as a separate and distinct race. Perceived as mixed-bloods or mulattoes, the Nanticokes at Indian River experienced the same cultural and spatial segregation accorded to Blacks. Among the White population there clearly existed considerable confusion about the origin and identity of the Nanticokes. In 1855, a court case in Sussex County, Delaware, drew attention to the social and racial status of the Nanticokes. Several years after the trial, George P. Fisher, the prosecuting attorney, detailed events of the case in *The So-Called Moors of Delaware* [53]. Levin Sockum, a successful Nanticoke landholder, was accused of violating a Delaware law that prohibited the sale or loan of firearms to a Negro or mulatto when he sold a quarter pound of powder and shot to Isaac Harman. Because Sockum had admitted to selling the powder and shot to Harman, Fisher had to demonstrate that Harman was indeed a mulatto. It is significant that none of the court's witnesses were able to establish Harman's ancestry. Fisher finally placed Lydia Clark, a blood relative of Harman, on the witness stand. Clark testified that before the American Revolution an Irish woman purchased and later married a light-colored slave. The offspring of this union intermarried with the remnant of the Nanticoke tribe. This testimony proved to the satisfaction of the court that Harman was a mulatto. Not only was Sockum found guilty and fined twenty dollars, he was brought into court on a second charge—possession of a gun. The court accepted testimony that Sockum was also a mulatto and fined him an additional twenty dollars. The verdicts rendered in the Harman and Sockum trials cemented the racial status and classification of the Nanticokes. For the remainder of the nineteenth century and well into the twentieth century, the Nanticokes were subjected to segregation in schooling, religious practices, residence, and social intercourse. Weslager's *Delaware's Forgotten Folk* [205] narrates the events of this significant period.

Indian Survivals in the East

Because most anthropologists and ethnologists pre-
ferred to visit Indian tribes west of the Mississippi
River, they were slow to recognize the presence of Indian survivals in the East. Initial interest among professional anthropologists in the possibility of surviving
Indian groups in the eastern United States began in
1889 when James Mooney distributed a questionnaire
about Indian survivals to one thousand local physicians
in certain counties of Maryland, Virginia, Delaware,
and North Carolina. On the Eastern Shore of Maryland and Virginia the replies to his letter indicated that
several groups still claimed descent from the Nanticoke, Piscataway, and Wicocomoco Indians. In 1898,
William H. Babcock with an unidentified companion
became the first professional anthropologist to visit
"The Nanticoke Indians of Indian River" [5]. In his
published report, Babcock discussed instances of
out-migration, the strong tendency toward endoga-
mous marriages, and the racial hostility that resulted in
the development of separate churches and schools.

One of the most influential scholars to address
seriously the question of Indian survivals in the eastern
United States was Frank G. Speck. Speck began his
fieldwork with the Nanticokes in 1911 and continued
to visit the community intermittently until his death in
1950. Speck's most significant contributions from his
work with "The Nanticoke Community of Delaware"

[170] rest in his gathering of ethnological specimens
and his recording of folklore, religion, and medicinal
cures. In particular Speck placed considerable emphasis on the activities and industries associated with the
production of corn. The cultivation of corn included
the use of suckering canes, corn-husking pegs, corn-
shellers, and large log corncribs that many local farm-
ers attributed to the Indians. Of equal importance were
the activities the Nanticokes devoted to marine life, because much of their subsistence was derived from the
Indian River. Speck's interviews with older informants
unearthed considerable information. "Back Again to
Indian River, Its People and Their Games" [173],
"'Cudgelling Rabbits,' an Old Nanticoke Hunting
Tradition and Its Significance" [176], "The Frolic
among the Nanticoke of Indian River Hundred, Delaware" [174], "A Maker of Eel-Pots among the Nanticokes of Delaware" [177], and "The Memorial Brush
Heap in Delaware and Elsewhere" [175] shed light on
folk remedies—especially burns, warts, measles, and
whooping cough—and made inquiries about children's
games, a theme long neglected by anthropologists. The
crossbow, popgun, arrow sling, stone sling, buzzer, and
bull-roarer all received attention.

　　Speck was also accustomed to taking his students
into the field for firsthand experience. One of the first
to join Speck in his work at Indian River was Gladys
Tantaquidgeon, of Mohegan descent, who collected
data about medical practices. Tantaquidgeon's material
on the Nanticokes was published in *A Study of Delaware*

Indian Medicine Practices and Folk Beliefs [188]. At a later date Anthony F. C. Wallace visited the community and outlined the possible investigation of the Nanticokes' historical and contemporary exploitation of the biota of Indian River and its banks [199].

Clinton A. Weslager also exhibited an avid interest in the Nanticokes of Indian River and the Moors of Cheswold, an offshoot of the Indian River community. This interest gave rise to a close friendship between Weslager and Speck, and with Speck's advice and criticism Weslager began fieldwork among the Moors and Nanticokes. Weslager's work resulted in the publication of *Delaware's Forgotten Folk: The Story of the Moors and Nanticokes* [205]. In addition, Weslager studied oral traditions, publishing "Folklore among the Nanticokes of Indian River Hundred and the Moors of Cheswold, Delaware" [213], "Folkways of the Nanticokes" [215], and "Nanticokes and the Buzzard Song" [208]. Frank W. Porter's "Anthropologists at Work: A Case Study of the Nanticoke Indian Community" [144] considers the influence of these studies and the presence of the investigators on the social organization of the community. Porter's *A Photographic Survey of Indian River Community* [143] provides a brief introductory essay and attempts to cover photographically the growth and development of the community.

Triracial Isolates

Prompted by investigations similar to those of Speck and Weslager, several individuals, during the 1930s and continuing to the present, became quite interested in the study of "mestizo," "mulatto," and "outcasted" groups in the eastern United States. It is critical to bear in mind that the interest of these researchers focused overwhelmingly on the social qualities and ramifications associated with these groups as triracial isolates, not necessarily as descendants of Indians. William H. Gilbert, who published "Memorandum concerning the Characteristics of the Larger Mixed-Blood Racial Islands of the Eastern United States" [62], "Surviving Indian Groups of the Eastern United States" [64], and *Synoptic Survey of Data on the Survival of Indian and Part Indian Blood in the Eastern United States* [63], attempted to enlist the interest and support of scientists and research foundations to investigate these groups. With reference to triracial isolates in Maryland and Delaware, considerable attention was directed to trends in the naming of mixed-blood populations [43]; analysis of the physical environment of their habitat [148]; social origins of the people [77]; estimation of admixture in racial hybrids [45]; patterns of mate selection [76] and [230]; and dental and medical findings of the people [226] and [156]. With little forethought, these authors aggregated all of the known surviving Indian groups of the eastern United States as mixed-blood racial islands.

Investigations framed solely within the context of triracial isolates have distorted our understanding of the essential processes involved in the persistence to the present of Indian survivals in Maryland and Delaware. The critical point to determine is the effect such perceptions have had on the emergence of these distinct communities and the development of their particular social institutions. Whether or not miscegenation can be biologically demonstrated, the Nanticokes and Piscataways and individuals outside their communities have reacted to this question in their own specific ways. During the nineteenth century and continuing well into the twentieth century, the question of the ethnic identity of the Nanticoke and Piscataway Indians has been brought to the fore on several occasions, forcing these communities to identify themselves officially as Indians or lose their separate identity forever.

This reaction to the classification as a triracial isolate clearly was significant in the social evolution and spatial development of the Nanticoke community at Indian River in Delaware. The reinvigoration of the Nanticoke community reflected a complex set of internal and external forces. The internal forces were in part residual culture traits from an earlier aboriginal period. Specifically, the strong desire to remain in their traditional habitat and maintain close kinship ties served to keep the remnant Indian population socially and spatially intact. External pressures reinforced this social cohesion. Primarily, the White population's subjection of the Nanticokes to the social status and classification of Negro or colored people strengthened and further hastened the development of the Indian River community because of the resulting separation of residences, enforcement of social distance from the Whites, and creation of separate social institutions, particularly churches and schools. These basic social institutions that were established during the middle decades of the nineteenth century have persisted, with the exception of the separate educational system, to the present.

ALPHABETICAL LIST AND INDEX

* Denotes items suitable for secondary school students

		Essay
Item		page
no.		no.

[1] Alsop, George A. 1666. *A Character of the Province of Maryland.* London: T. J. Dring. New ed., New York: W. Gowans, 1869; Cleveland: Burrows Brothers, 1902. Reprinted, Bainbridge, N.Y.: York Mail-Print, 1972 (1869 ed.); Freeport, N.Y.: Books for Libraries Press, 1972 (1902 ed.). (25)

[2] Andrews, Matthew Page 1929. *History of Maryland: Province and State.* New York: Doubleday, Doran. Reprinted, Hatboro, Pa.: Tradition Press, 1965. (4)

[3] ———. 1933. *The Founding of Maryland.* Baltimore: Williams and Wilkins; New York and London: Appleton-Century. (4)

[4] Arber, Edward, ed. 1910. *Travels and Works of Captain John Smith, President of*

*Virginia and Admiral of New England,
1580–1631.* 2 vols. Edinburgh: John
Grant.   (20, 27, 38)

[5]   Babcock, William H. 1899. "The Nanticoke Indians of Indian River." *American Anthropologist,* N.S., 1:277–82.   (50)

[6]   Bacon, Thomas. 1765. *Laws of Maryland
at Large, with Proper Indexes, Now First
Collected into one Compleat Body, and Pub-
lished from the Original Acts and Records,
Remaining in the Secretary's Office of the
Said Province. Together with Notes and
Other Matters, Relative to the Constitution
Thereof, Extracted from the Provincial Rec-
ords. To Which Is Prefixed, the Charter with
an English Translation.* Annapolis: Jonas
Green.   (1)

[7]   Baer, Elizabeth. 1949. *Seventeenth Century Maryland: A Bibliography.* Introduction by Lawrence C. Wroth. Baltimore:
John Work Garrett Library.   (3)

[8]   Beardsley, Gretchen. 1939. "The
Groundnut as Used by the Indians of
Eastern North America." *Michigan*

Academy of Science, Arts and Letters 25:507–15. (28)

[9] Beauchamp, William M. 1916. *Moravian Journals Relating to Central New York, 1745–66.* Syracuse: Dehler Press for the Onondaga Historical Association. Reprinted, New York: AMS, 1976. (46)

[10] Beitzell, Edwin W. 1959. *The Jesuit Missions of St. Mary's County, Maryland.* Abell, Md.: Published by the author. 2d ed., 1976. (40)

[11] Bender, Harry E. 1929. "The Nanticoke Indians in Lancaster County." Lancaster County Historical Society, *Historical Papers and Addresses* 33:121–30. (46)

[12] Berry, Brewton. 1963. *Almost White: A Study of Certain Racial Hybrids in the Eastern United States.* New York: Macmillan. Reprinted, London and New York: Collier-Macmillan, 1969. (xv)

[13] Blackman, M. James. 1976. "The Geochemical Analysis of Jasper Ar-

tifacts and Source Material from Delaware and Pennsylvania." In *Transactions of the Delaware Academy of Science,* ed. John C. Kraft, 5–6:37–48. Newark: Delaware Academy of Science.   (30)

[14]   Blaker, Margaret C. 1950. "Pottery Types from the Townsend Site, Lewes, Delaware." *Bulletin, Eastern States Archeological Federation* 9(July): 11.   (12)

[15]   Bozman, John Leeds. 1837. *The History of Maryland, from Its First Settlement, in 1633, to the Restoration, in 1660, with a Copious Introduction, and Notes and Illustrations.* 2 vols. Baltimore: J. Lucas and E. K. Deaver. Reprinted, Spartansburg, S.C.: Reprint Company, 1968.   (4)

[16]   Brennan, Louis A. 1970. "A Further Definition of Stephenson's Middle Atlantic Seaboard Culture Province." *Bulletin, Eastern States Archeological Federation* 29(July):9.   (19)

[17]   Brew, John Otis. 1943. *A Selected Bibliography of American Indian Archaeology East of the Rocky Mountains.* Cambridge, Mass.: Excavator's Club.   (2)

[18]   Bump, Charles W. 1907. "Indian
       Place-Names in Maryland." *Maryland
       Historical Magazine* 2(December):287–
       93.   (32)

[19]   Bushnell, David I. 1940. "The Use of
       Soapstone by the Indians of the Eastern
       United States." *Annual Report of the
       Board of Regents of the Smithsonian In-
       stitution for 1939*, pp. 471–89. Washing-
       ton, D.C.: Smithsonian Institution.   (30)

[20]   Cadzow, Donald A. 1936. "Archaeolog-
       ical Studies of the Susquehannock In-
       dians of Pennsylvania." *Publications of
       the Pennsylvania Historical Commission* 3.
       Harrisburg: Pennsylvania Historical
       Commission.   (25)

[21]   Campbell, B. U. 1906. "Early Missions
       among the Indians in Maryland."
       Maryland Historical Magazine
       1(December):293–316.   (40)

[22]   Clark, Charles Branch. 1950. *The East-
       ern Shore of Maryland and Virginia*. New
       York: Lewis Historical Publishing
       Company.   (5)

[23]   Clark, Wayne E. 1976. "The Application of Regional Research Designs to Contract Archaeology: The Northwest Transportation Corridor Archaeological Survey Project." M.A. thesis, American University.   (13)

[24]   Clayton, Sarah. 1973. "The Potomac (Patawomeke) Indians." *Quarterly Bulletin, Archaeological Society of Virginia* 27:177–89.   (26)

[25]   Cooper, Peter P. 1972. "The Southeastern Archaeological Area Re-defined." *Quarterly Bulletin, Archaeological Society of Virginia* 26:136–44.   (18)

[26]   Covington, Harry F. 1915. "The Discovery of Maryland; or, Verrazano's Visit to the Eastern Shore." *Maryland Historical Magazine* 10:199–217.   (37)

[27]   Cresson, Hilborne T. 1892. *Report upon Pile Structures in Naaman's Creek, Near Claymont, Delaware.* Archaeological and Ethnological Papers of the Peabody Museum 1. Reprinted, New York: Kraus, 1974.   (6)

[28] Crozier, A. 1947. "Fishing Methods of the Indians of the Delmarva Region." *Bulletin of the Archaeological Society of Delaware* 4:16–19. (29)

[29] Cumming, William P., S. E. Hillier, David B. Quinn, and G. Williams. 1974. *The Exploration of North America, 1630–1776.* London: P. Elek; Toronto: McClelland and Stewart; New York: G. P. Putnam's Sons. (37)

[30] Cumming, William P., Raleigh A. Skelton, and David B. Quinn. 1971. *The Discovery of North America.* London: P. Elek. New ed., New York: American Heritage Press, 1972. (37)

[31] Dalrymple, E. A., ed. 1874. *Relatio Itineris in Marylandiam Declaratio Coloniae Domini Baronis de Baltimoro ad Annum 1638. . . . Narrative of a Voyage to Maryland, by Father Andrew White, S.J. An Account of the Colony of the Lord Baron of Baltimore. Extracts from Different Letters of Missionaries, from the Year 1635 to the Year 1677.* Fund Publication 7. Baltimore: Maryland Historical Society. (40)

[32]   Davidson, D. S. 1934. "Problems in the Archaeology of the Delmarva Peninsula." *Bulletin of the Archaeological Society of Delaware* 1:1–8.   (8)

[33]   ———. 1935. "Burial Customs in the Delmarva Peninsula and the Question of Their Chronology." *American Antiquity* 1:84–97.   (10)

[34]   DeLaBarre, Reamor Robin. 1958. "Chesapeake Bay Indian Population." M.A. thesis, Johns Hopkins University.   (35)

[35]   Delaware (Colony) General Assembly. 1929. *Minutes of the House of Assembly of the Government of the Counties of New Castle, Kent and Sussex upon Delaware at Sessions Held at New Castle in the year 1739.* Wilmington: Printed for the Public Archives Commission of Delaware.   (1)

[36]   ———. 1929. *Minutes of the House of Assembly of the Three Counties upon Delaware at Sessions Held at New Castle in the Years 1740–1742.* Wilmington: Printed for the Public Archives Commission of Delaware.   (1)

[37] Denevan, William M., ed. 1976. *The Native Population of the Americas in 1492.* Madison: University of Wisconsin Press. (35)

[38] De Valinger, Leon. 1941. *Indian Land Sales in Delaware with Addendum: A Discussion of the Family Hunting Territory Question in Delaware.* Wilmington: Wilmington Press for the Archaeological Society of Delaware. (xiv, 45)

[39] Dobyns, Henry F. 1966. "Estimating Aboriginal American Population: An Appraisal of Techniques with a New Hemispheric Estimate." *Current Anthropology* 7:395–416. (34)

[40] ———. 1976. *Native American Historical Demography: A Critical Bibliography.* Center for the History of the American Indian Bibliographical Series. Bloomington: Indiana University Press for the Newberry Library. (35)

[41] Driver, Harold E. 1961. *Indians of North America.* Chicago: University of Chicago Press. 2d ed. rev., 1969. Reprinted, 1973. (18)

[42]   Dunlap, Arthur R. 1949. "A Biblio-
graphical Discussion of the Indian
Languages of the Delmarva Peninsula."
*Bulletin of the Archaeological Society of
Delaware* 4:2–5.   (31)

[43]   Dunlap, Arthur R., and Clinton A.
Weslager. 1947. "Trends in the Naming
of Tri-Racial Mixed-Blood Groups in
the Eastern United States." *American
Speech* 22:81–87.   (53)

[44]   ———. 1950. *Indian Place-Names in
Delaware*. Wilmington: Archaeological
Society of Delaware.   (32)

[45]   Elston, R. C. 1971. "The Estimation of
Admixture in Racial Hybrids." *Annals of
Human Genetics* 35:9–17.   (53)

[46]   Emory, Frederic. 1950. *Queen Anne's
County, Maryland, Its Early History and
Development: A Series of Sketches Based
upon Original Research*. Baltimore: Maryland Historical Society.   (4)

[47]   Evans, Clifford. 1955. *A Ceramic Study
of Virginia Archeology: With Appendix, an*

Analysis of Projectile Points and Large Blades, by C. G. Holland. United States Bureau of American Ethnology Bulletin 160. Washington, D.C.: Government Printing Office.   (11, 19)

[48]   Feest, Christian. 1978. "The Nanticokes and Neighboring Tribes." In *Northeast,* ed. Bruce G. Trigger, pp. 240–52. Vol. 15 of *Handbook of North American Indians,* gen. ed. William C. Sturtevant. 20 vols. 1978–. Washington, D.C.: Government Printing Office for the Smithsonian Institution.   (22)

[49]   Ferguson, Alice Leczinska L. 1937. "Burial Area in Moyaone." *Journal of the Washington Academy of Sciences* 27:261–67.   (10)

[50]   ———. 1937. *Moyaone and the Piscataway Indians.* Washington, D.C.: Published by the author.   (9, 23)

[51]   ———. 1940. "An Ossuary Near Piscataway Creek with a Report on the Skeletal Remains by T. D. Stewart." *American Antiquity* 6:4–18.   (10)

[52]   Ferguson, Alice Leczinska L., and
        Henry G. Ferguson. 1960. *The Piscata-*
        way Indians of Southern Maryland. Ac-
        cokeek, Md.: Alice Ferguson Foundation.   (23)

[53]   Fisher, George P. N.d. *The So-Called*
        Moors of Delaware. Dover, Del.: N.p.
        Also appeared in the *Milford Delaware*
        Herald, 15 June, 1895.   (49)

[54]   Flannery, Regina. 1939. *An Analysis of*
        Coastal Algonquian Culture. Catholic
        University of America Anthropological
        Series 7. Washington, D.C.: Catholic
        University of American Press.   (28)

[55]   Fleet, Henry. 1876. "A Brief Journal of
        a Voyage Made in the Bark 'Warwick' to
        Virginia and Other Parts of the Conti-
        nent of America." In *The Founders of*
        Maryland as Portrayed in Manuscripts,
        Provincial Records and Early Documents,
        ed. Edward D. Neill, pp. 19–37. Al-
        bany: Joel Munsell.   (38)

[56]   Fogelson, Raymond D., ed. Forthcom-
        ing. *The Southeast.* Vol. 14 of *Handbook*
        of North American Indians, gen. ed.

William C. Sturtevant. 20 vols. 1978–.
Washington, D.C.: Government Printing
Office for the Smithsonian Institution.   (21)

[57]   Fowke, Gerard. 1896. "Stone Art." In
*Thirteenth Annual Report of the United
States Bureau of American Ethnology,*
1891–92, pp. 47–178. Washington,
D.C.: Government Printing Office.   (7)

[58]   Gallatin, Albert. 1836. *A Synopsis of the
Indian Tribes within the United States East
of the Rocky Mountains and in the British
and Russian Possessions in North America.*
Archaeologica Americana 2. Cambridge, Mass.: American Antiquarian
Society. Reprinted, New York: AMS,
1973.   (20)

[59]   Gardner, William M., and Charles W.
McNett. 1971. "Early Pottery in the
Potomac." *First Middle Atlantic Ar-
chaeological Conference,* pp. 42–52. N.p.:
N.p.   (13)

[60]   Gifford, George E., and Marion Tingling. 1958. "A Relation of a Voyage to
the Head of the Bay." *The Historian*
20(May):347–51.   (38)

[61]   Gilbert, William H. 1945. "The Wesorts of Southern Maryland: An Outcasted Group." *Journal of the Washington Academy of Sciences* 35(August):237–46.   (24)

[62]   ———. 1946. "Memorandum concerning the Characteristics of the Larger Mixed-Blood Racial Islands of the Eastern United States." *Social Forces* 34(May):438–47.   (53)

[63]   ———. 1947. *Synoptic Survey of Data on the Survival of Indian and Part Indian Blood in the Eastern United States.* Washington, D.C.: Library of Congress, Legislative Reference Service.   (53)

[64]   ———. 1949. "Surviving Indian Groups of the Eastern United States." *Annual Report of the Smithsonian Institution for 1948,* pp. 407–38. Washington, D.C.: Government Printing Office.   (53)

[65]   Goddard, Ives. 1978. "Eastern Algonquian Languages." In *Northeast,* ed. Bruce G. Trigger, pp. 70–77. Vol. 15 of *Handbook of North American Indians,* gen. ed. William C. Sturtevant. 20 vols.

1978–. Washington, D.C.: Government Printing Office for the Smithsonian Institution. (31)

[66] Graham, William J. 1935. *The Indians of Port Tobacco River, Maryland, and Their Burial Places.* Washington, D.C.: Published by the author. (26)

[67] Greeneville, Sir Richard. 1589. "An Account of the Particularities of the Imployments of the English Men Left in Virginia by Sir Richard Greeneville under the Charge of Master Ralph Lane Generall of the Same, from the 17 of August 1585 until the 18 of June 1586 at Which Time They Departed the Country." In *The Principall Navigations, Voiages and Discoveries of the English Nation . . . ,* ed. Richard Hakluyt. London: George Bishop, Ralph Newberie and Robert Barker. Reprinted, Cambridge: Cambridge University Press for the Hakluyt Society and the Peabody Museum, 1965. (27)

[68] Griffin, James B. 1946. "Cultural Changes and Continuity in Eastern

United States Archaeology." In *Man in the Northeastern United States*, ed. Frederick Johnson, pp. 37–95. Andover, Mass.: Phillips Academy.   (15)

[69]   Griffith, Daniel R. 1976. "Ecological Studies of Prehistory." In *Transactions of the Delaware Academy of Science*, ed. John C. Kraft, 5–6:63–81. Newark: Delaware Academy of Science.   (27)

[70]   ———. 1977. "Townsend Ceramics in the Late Woodland of Southern Delaware." M.A. thesis, American University.   (12)

[71]   Griffith, Daniel R., and Richard E. Artusy. 1975. "A Brief Report of Semi-subterranean Dwellings on the Delmarva Peninsula." *Archeolog* 27:1–9.   (13)

[72]   Guthe, Alfred K., and Patricia B. Kelley. 1963. *An Anthropological Bibliography of the Eastern Seaboard*. Trenton: Eastern States Archaeological Federation.   (2)

[73]   Hall, Clayton C., ed. 1910. *Narratives of Early Maryland, 1633–1684*. Original

Narratives of Early American History Series, ed. John F. Jameson. New York: Scribners. Reprinted, N.Y.: Barnes and Noble, 1946; Louisville: Lost Cause Press, 1960.   (1)

[74] Hancock, James E. 1927. "The Indians of the Chesapeake Bay Section." *Maryland Historical Magazine* 22(March:23–40.   (20)

[75] Hanson, George Adolphus. 1876. *Old Kent: The Eastern Shore of Maryland; Notes Illustrative of the Most Ancient Records of Kent County, Maryland and of the Parishes of St. Pauls, Shrewbury and I. U.* . . . Baltimore: John P. Des Forges. Reprinted, Baltimore: Regional Publishing Company, 1967.   (3)

[76] Harte, Thomas J. 1959. "Trends in Mate Selection in a Tri-Racial Isolate." *Social Forces* 37(March):215–21.   (53)

[77] ———. 1963. "Social Origins of the Brandywine Population." *Phylon* 24:369–78.   (53)

[78]   Heckewelder, John G. E. 1822. *Histoire, mours et coutumes des nations indiennes qui habitaient autrefois la Pennsylvanie et les états voisins.* Paris: L. de Bure. Reprinted in English as *History, Manners and Customs of the Indian Nations Who Once Inhabited Pennsylvania and the Neighboring States.* Memoirs of the Historical Society of Pennsylvania 12. Philadelphia: Historical Society of Pennsylvania, 1876. Rev. ed., notes and intro. Rev. William C. Reichel, 1881. Reprint of 1876 ed., New York: Arno, 1971.   (21, 42)

[79]   Henry, Jane. 1970. "The Choptank Indians of Maryland under the Proprietary Government." *Maryland Historical Magazine* 65 (Summer): 171–80.   (26, 43)

[80]   Hobbs, Horace P. 1961. *Pioneers of the Potowmack, Beinge a Brief Historie of ye Discoverie and Explorations of ye River Patawomeke, Containing ye True and Remarkable Adventures of Certain Bold Mariners, Missionaries, Traders, Settlers, and Rangers That Ventured into ye Remotest Parts of That River, and What Dangers, Warrs, and Strange Occurrences Befell Them amongst ye Wilde and Salvage In-*

dians Thereof. Washington, D.C.: Published by the author. 2d ed. published by the author, 1964. (4)

[81]   Hodge, Frederick Webb, ed. 1907–10. *Handbook of American Indians North of Mexico.* United States Bureau of American Ethnology Bulletin 30. 2 vols. Washington, D.C.: Government Printing Office for the Smithsonian Institution. Reprinted, New York: Pageant, 1959; New York: Rowman and Littlefield, 1965, 1971; Grosse Pointe, Mich.: Scholarly, 1968; Totowa, N.J.: Rowman and Littlefield, 1975. (21, 33)

[82]   Hoffman, Bernard G. 1967. "Ancient Tribes Revisited: A Summary of Indian Distribution and Movement in the Northeastern United States from 1534 to 1779. Parts 1–3." *Ethnohistory* 14(Winter/Spring): 1–46. (21)

[83]   Holmes, William H. 1897. "Stone Implements of the Potomac-Chesapeake Tidewater Province." In *Fifteenth Annual Report of the United States Bureau of American Ethnology, 1893–4,* pp. 3–152. Washington, D.C.: Government Printing Office. (8)

[84]   ———. 1903. "Aboriginal Pottery of the Eastern United States." In *Twentieth Annual Report of the United States Bureau of American Ethnology*, 1898–90, pp. 1–237. Washington, D.C.: Government Printing Office.   (7)

[85]   ———. 1914. "Areas of American Culture Classification Tentatively Outlined as an Aid in the Study of the Antiquities." *American Anthropologist* 16:413–46.   (17)

[86]   Humphrey, Robert L., and Mary Elizabeth Chambers. 1977. *Ancient Washington: American Indian Cultures of the Potomac Valley*. GW Washington Studies 6. Washington, D.C.: George Washington University.   (24)

[87]   Hunter, William A. 1969. "The Historic Role of the Susquehannocks." In *Susquehannock Miscellany*, ed. John Witthoft and W. Fred Kinsey, pp. 8–18. Harrisburg: Pennsylvania Historical and Museum Commission.   (25)

[88]   Hutchinson, Henry H. 1961. "Indian

Reservations of the Maryland Provincial Assembly on the Middle Delmarva Peninsula." *Archeolog* 13(October):1–5.   (43)

[89] Hutchinson, Henry H., and David Marine. 1962. "Further Information Re. Soapstone Bowls, Quarries and Artifacts." *Archeolog* 14(March):1–11.   (30)

[90] Isaac, Erich. 1957. "Kent Island, Part I: The Period of Settlement." *Maryland Historical Magazine* 52:93–119.   (4)

[91] Jennings, Francis. 1966. "The Indian Trade of the Susquehanna Valley." *Proceedings of the American Philosophical Society* 110(December):406–24.   (25)

[92] ———. 1968. "Glory, Death and Transfiguration: The Susquehannock Indians in the Seventeenth Century." *Proceedings of the American Philosophical Society* 112(January):15–53.   (25)

[93] Johnston, Charles M., ed. 1964. *The Valley of the Six Nations: A Collection of Documents on the Indian Lands of the Grand*

River. Toronto: University of Toronto
Press.   (46)

[94]   Johnston, George. 1881. *The History of
Cecil County, Maryland, and the Early Set-
tlements around the Head of Chesapeake
Bay and on the Delaware River, with
Sketches of Some of the Old Families of Cecil
County.* Elkton: Published by the
author. Reprinted, Baltimore: Regional
Publishing Company, 1967, 1972.   (4)

[95]   Jones, Elias. 1925. *Revised History of
Dorchester County, Maryland.* Baltimore:
Read-Taylore Press. Reprinted, Cam-
bridge, Mass.: Tidewater Press, 1966.   (4)

[96]   Jordan, Francis. 1906. *Aboriginal Fishing
Stations on the Coast of the Middle Atlantic
States.* Lancaster, Pa.: New Era Printing
Company.   (29)

[97]   Kenny, Hamill T. 1961. *The Origin and
Meaning of the Indian Place Names of
Maryland.* Baltimore: Waverly Press.   (32)

[98]   Kent, Barry C. 1970. "Conoy Town on
the Lower Susquehanna River, 1718–

1743." *Bulletin, Eastern States Archaeological Federation* 30:13.   (46)

[99]   Kilty, John. 1808. *The Land-holder's Assistant, and Land-Office Guide; Being an Exposition of Original Titles, as Derived from the Proprietary Government, and More Recently from the State of Maryland; Designed to Explain the Manner in Which Such Titles Have Been, and May Be Acquired and Completed.* Baltimore: G. Dobbin and Murphy.   (42)

[100] Kinsey, W. Fred. 1971. "The Middle Atlantic Culture Province: A Point of View." *Pennsylvania Archaeologist* 41(April):1–8.   (19)

[101] Kraft, John C., ed. 1976. "The Pre-European Archaeology of Delaware." *Transactions of the Delaware Academy of Science*, vol. 5. Newark: Delaware Academy of Science.   (xviii)

[102] Kroeber, Alfred L. 1939. *Cultural and Natural Areas of Native North America.* University of California Publications in American Archaeology and Ethnology

38. Berkeley: University of California Press. Reprinted, Millwood, N.Y.: Kraus, 1976.   (18, 34)

[103] Landis, David H. 1929. *A Brief Description of Indian Life and Indian Trade of the Susquehannock Indians, the Tribe Which Inhabited What Is Now Lancaster County, Pennsylvania: A Compilation of Pen Pictures by the Earliest Europeans with Whom They Came in Contact. Also Giving a Study of the Exact Location and Period of Occupation of Their Villages and Fort Sites Based on the Articles Found in Indian Graves Here.* . . . Lancaster, Pa.: N.p. Reprinted from the *Lancaster New Era,* 22 June 1929.   (25)

[104] ———. 1933. "Conoy Indian Town and Peter Bezaillon." In *Papers Read before the Lancaster County Historical Society* 37:113–36.   (46)

[105] Le May, Joseph A. 1972. *Men of Letters in Colonial Maryland.* Knoxville: University of Tennessee Press.   (40)

[106] Lewis, Clifford M., and Albert J.

Loomie. 1953. *The Spanish Jesuit Mission in Virginia, 1570–1572.* Chapel Hill: University of North Carolina Press.   (39)

[107] Loskiel, George H. 1794. *History of the Mission of the United Brethren among the Indians in North America.* London: Brethren's Society for the Furtherance of the Gospel.   (42)

[108] Lowdermilk, William H. 1878. *History of Cumberland (Maryland), from the time of the Indian town Caiuctucuk, in 1728, up to the Present Day, Embracing an Account of Washington's First Campaign and Battle of Fort Necessity, Together with a History of Braddock's Expedition,* Washington, D.C.: James Anglim. Reprinted, Baltimore: Regional Publishing Company, 1971.   (4)

[109] McKern, W. C. 1946. "A Cultural Perspective of Northeastern Area Archaeology." In *Man in Northeastern North America,* ed. Frederick Johnson, pp. 33–36. Andover, Mass.: Phillips Academy.   (14, 15)

[110] MacLeod, William Christie. 1922. "The

Family Hunting Territory and Lenape Political Organization." *American Anthropologist* 24:448–63.   (45)

[111]   ———. 1926. "Piscataway Royalty: A Study in Stone Age Government and Inheritance Rulings." *Journal of the Washington Academy of Sciences* 16(June):301–9.   (23)

[112]   ———. 1928. *The American Indian Frontier.* London: K. Paul, Trench, Trubner and Company. New York: Alfred Knopf. Reprinted, London: Dawson's of Pall Mall, 1968.   (34)

[113]   McMahon, John V. L. 1831. *An Historical View of the Government of Maryland, from Its Colonization to the Present Day.* Baltimore: F. Lucas, Jr., and Cushing and Sons, and W. J. Neal.   (5)

[114]   McNett, Charles W., and William M. Gardner. 1971. "Shell Middens of the Potomac Coastal Plain." *First Middle Atlantic Archaeological Conference,* pp. 21–31. N.p.:N.p.   (13)

[115]   McSherry, James. 1849. *History of Maryland: From Its First Settlement in 1634, to the Year 1848.* Baltimore: John Murphy. Revised ed., Baltimore: Baltimore Book Company, 1904. Reprinted (1904 ed.), Spartansburg, S.C.: Reprint Company, 1968.   (4)

[116]   Manson, Carl. 1948. "Marcey Creek Site: An Early Manifestation in the Potomac Valley." *American Antiquity* 13:223–27.   (9)

[117]   Marye, Wm. B. 1935. "Piscattaway." *Maryland Historical Magazine* 30(September):183–240.   (23)

[118]   ———. 1936. "Former Indian Sites in Maryland as Located by Early Colonial Records." *American Antiquity* 2:40–46.   (xiv)

[119]   ———. 1936–30. "Indian Paths of Delmarva Peninsula." *Bulletin of the Archaeological Society of Delaware* 2(March 1936):5–22; 2(October 1936):5–27; 2(October 1937):1–25; 2(June 1938):4–11.   (xiv)

[120]   ———. 1937. "Burial Methods in
Maryland and Adjacent States." *American Antiquity* 2:209–14.   (10)

[121]   ———. 1938. "The Wiccomiss Indians
of Maryland." *American Antiquity*
4:146–52.   (26)

[122]   ———. 1940. *Indian Towns of the South-
eastern Part of Sussex County, Delaware.*
Wilmington: Archaeological Society of
Delaware.   (xiv)

[123]   [Maryland, Archives of]. 1883–. *Archives of Maryland,* ed. William H.
Browne, et al. 72 vols. to date. Baltimore: Maryland Historical Society.   (xiv, 1,
                                        23, 43)

[124]   Maryland General Assembly. 1853. *Report of the Select Committee on the Claims of
the Nanticoke Indians, Made to the House
of Delegates.* Annapolis: Thomas E.
Martin.   (47)

[125]   [Maryland, Laws of]. 1777–. *Laws of
Maryland, made and passed at a session of
Assembly,* (Title and publisher vary ac-
cording to year).   (1)

[126] Maxwell, Hu. 1910. "The Use and Abuse of Forests by the Virginia Indians." *William and Mary Quarterly Historical Magazine* 19:73–104. (28)

[127] Mercer, Henry C. 1897. "The Discovery of Aboriginal Remains at a Rock Shelter in the Delaware Valley known as the Indian House." In *Researches upon the Antiquity of Man in the Delaware Valley and the Eastern United States,* ed. H. C. Mercer, E. D. Cope, and R. H. Harte, pp. 139–47. Boston: Ginn. See [129]. (6)

[128] ———. 1897. "Exploration of an Indian Ossuary on the Choptank River, Dorchester County, Maryland." In *Researches upon the Antiquity of Man in the Delaware Valley and the Eastern United States,* ed. H. C. Mercer, E. D. Cope, and R. H. Harte, pp. 87–109. Boston: Ginn. See [129]. (6)

[129] Mercer, Henry C., Edward D. Cope, and R. H. Harte. 1897. *Researches upon the Antiquity of Man in the Delaware Valley and the Eastern United States.* University of Pennsylvania Publications in Philology, Literature and Archaeology, No. 6. Boston: Ginn. (6)

[130]   Moeller, Roger W., and John Reid.
1977. *Archaeological Bibliography for Eastern North America*. New Haven: Eastern
States Archeological Federation and
American Indian Archaeological Institute.   (2)

[131]   Mooney, James. 1889. "Indian Tribes
of the District of Columbia." *American
Anthropologist* 2:259–66.   (20)

[132]   ———. 1928. *The Aboriginal Population
of America North of Mexico*, ed. John R.
Swanton. Smithsonian Miscellaneous
Collections 80(7). Washington, D.C.:
Smithsonian Institution.   (33)

[133]   Moorehead, Warren K. 1910. *The Stone
Age in North America: An Archaeological
Encyclopedia of the Implements, Ornaments,
Weapons, Utensils, Etc., of the Prehistoric
Tribes of North America*. 2 vols. Boston
and New York: Houghton Mifflin.   (8)

[134]   Murdock, George P. 1941. *Ethnographic
Bibliography of North America*. New Haven: Yale University Press. 2d ed., New
Haven: Human Relations Area Files,
1953. 4th ed., coauthored with

Timothy J. O'Leary, 5 vols., New Haven: Human Relations Area Files, 1975. (2)

[135] "Narrative of a Voyage to Maryland, 1705–1706." [1907]. *American Historical Review* 12:327–40. (28)

[136] Norwood, Henry. [1650]. "A Voyage to Virginia." In *Tracts and Other Papers Relating Principally to the Origin, Settlement and Progress of the Colonies in North America, from the Discovery of the Country to the Year 1776,* ed. Peter Force. 4 vols. Washington, D.C.: Peter Force, 1836–46. Reprinted, New York: Peter Smith, 1947; Gloucester, Mass.: Peter Smith, 1963. (38)

[137] Omwake, H. Geiger, and T. D. Stewart, eds. 1963. "The Townsend Site Near Lewes, Delaware." *Archeolog,* vol. 15. (12)

[138] [Pennsylvania Archives]. 1851–53. *Minutes of the Provincial Council of Pennsylvania from the Organization to the Termination of the Proprietary Government,* ed. Samuel Hazard, et al. 16 vols.

Philadelphia and Harrisburg: Joseph
Severns and Theodore Fenn.   (1)

[139]   ———. 1852–56. *Pennsylvania Archives,*
ed. Samuel Hazard. 12 vols. Philadelphia: Joseph Severns for the State of
Pennsylvania.   (1)

[140]   ———. 1860. *General Index to the Co-
lonial Records, in 16 Volumes, and to the
Pennsylvania Archives, in 12 Volumes,* ed.
Samuel Hazard. Philadelphia: Joseph
Severns. Reprinted, New York: AMS,
1976.   (46)

[141]   ———. 1949. *Guide to the Published
Archives of Pennsylvania,* ed. Martha L.
Simonetti. Harrisburg: Pennsylvania
Historical and Museum Commission,
Commonwealth of Pennsylvania. Re-
printed, 1976.   (See [139])

[142]   Pilling, James C. 1891. *Bibliography of
the Algonquian Language.* United States
Bureau of American Ethnology Bulletin 13. Washington, D.C.: Government
Printing Office.   (31)

[143]   Porter, Frank W., III. 1977. *A Photographic Survey of Indian River Community.* Millsboro: Indian Mission Church.   (52)

[144]   ———. 1978. "Anthropologists at Work: A Case Study of the Nanticoke Indian Community." *American Indian Quarterly* 4(February):1–18.   (52)

[145]   ———. 1979. "A Century of Accommodation: The Nanticokes in Colonial Maryland." *Maryland Historical Magazine,* vol. 74(Summer): 175–92.   (22, 41)

[146]   ———. 1979. "Strategies for Survival: The Nanticokes in a Hostile World." *Ethnohistory,* vol. 26(Spring).   (43, 47)

[147]   Powell, John Wesley. 1891. *Indian Linguistic Families of America, North of Mexico.* Seventh Annual Report of the United States Bureau of American Ethnology. Washington, D.C.: Government Printing Office.   (17)

[148]   Price, Edward T. 1953. "A Geographic Analysis of White-Indian-Negro Racial

Mixtures in the Eastern United States."
*Annals of the Association of American
Geographers* 43:138–55.   (53)

[149]   Quinn, David Beers, comp. 1971. *North
American Discovery circa 1000–1612.*
New York: Harper and Row.   (36)

[150]   ———. 1977. *North America from Ear-
liest Discovery to First Settlements: The
Norse Voyages to 1612.* New York:
Harper and Row.   (36)

[151]   Reynolds, Elmer R. 1880. "Aboriginal
Soapstone Quarries in the District of
Columbia." In *Twelfth Annual Report of
the Trustees of the Peabody Museum of
American Archaeology and Ethnology*
2:526–35.   (30)

[152]   ———. 1889. "Memoirs on the Pre-
Columbian Shell Mounds at Newburg,
Maryland and the Aboriginal Shell
Mounds of the Potomac and the
Wicomico Rivers." *American An-
thropologist* 2:252–59.   (7)

[153]   Ritchie, William A. 1946. "Archaeological Manifestations and Relative Chronology in the Northeast." In *Man in Northeastern North America,* ed. Frederick Johnson, pp. 96–105. Andover, Mass.: Phillips Academy.   (15)

[154]   Rouse, Irving. 1947. *An Anthropological Bibliography of the Eastern Seaboard.* 2 vols. New Haven: Eastern States Archeological Federation.   (2)

[155]   Royce, Charles C., comp. 1896–97. *Indian Land Cessions in the United States.* Eighteenth Annual Report of the United States Bureau of American Ethnology. Washington, D.C.: Government Printing Office. Reissued, 1899. Reprinted, New York: Arno, 1971; New York: AMS, 1973.   (42)

[156]   Rucknagel, D. L. 1964. "The Gene for Sickle Cell Hemoglobin in the Wesorts: An Extreme Example of Genetic Drift and the Founder Effect." Ph.D. diss., University of Michigan.   (53)

[157]   Schaeffer, Claude E., and Leo J.

Roland. 1941. *A Partial Bibliography of the Archaeology of Pennsylvania and Adjacent States.* Harrisburg: Pennsylvania Historical Commission.   (2)

[158]   Scharf, John T. 1879. *History of Maryland, from the Earliest Period to the Present Day.* Baltimore: J. B. Piet. Reprinted, Hatboro, Pa.: Tradition Press, 1967.   (3)

[159]   ———. 1882. *History of Western Maryland; Being a History of Frederick, Montgomery, Carroll, Washington, Allegany and Garrett Counties from the Earliest Period to Present Day.* Philadelphia: Louis H. Everts. Reprinted, Baltimore: Regional Publishing Company, 1968.   (3)

[160]   ———. 1888. *History of Delaware, 1609–1888.* Philadelphia: L. J. Richards. Reprinted, Port Washington, N.Y.: Kennikat Press, 1972.   (3)

[161]   Schmitt, Karl. 1952. "Archaeological Chronology of the Middle Atlantic States." In *Archeology of the Eastern United States,* ed. James Griffin, pp. 59–70. Chicago: University of Chicago Press.   (11, 18)

[162] Schoolcraft, Henry Rowe. 1857. *History of the Indian Tribes of the United States: Their Present Condition and Prospects, and a Sketch of Their Ancient Status.* Vol. 6 of *Historical and Statistical Information Respecting the History, Condition and Prospects of the Indian Tribes of the United States.* 6 vols. Philadelphia: Lippincott, Grambo, 1851–57. Republished as *Archives of Aboriginal Knowledge.* 6 vols. Philadelphia: J. B. Lippincott, 1860. Index comp. by Francis S. Nichols. Washington, D.C.: Government Printing Office, 1954. Reprint of entire work including index under series title, *Historical and Statistical Information.* . . . 7 vols. New York: AMS, 1969. (20)

[163] Scisco, Louis D. 1945. "Discovery of the Chesapeake Bay, 1525–1573." *Maryland Historical Magazine* 40:277–86. (38)

[164] ———. 1947. "Voyage of Vincente Gonzalez in 1588." *Maryland Historical Magazine* 42:95–100. (38)

[165] Semmes, Raphael. 1929. "Aboriginal Maryland, 1608–1689. Part One: The Eastern Shore." *Maryland Historical Maga-*

zine 24(June):157–72; "Aboriginal Maryland, 1608–1689. Part Two: The Western Shore." Ibid., 24(September):195–209.   (35)

[166]   ———. 1937. *Captains and Mariners of Early Maryland*. Baltimore: Johns Hopkins University Press.   (xiv)

[167]   Shea, John G. 1855. *History of the Catholic Missions among the Indian Tribes of the United States, 1529–1854*. New York: Edward Dunigan and Brothers. Reprinted, New York: Arno, 1969.   (40)

[168]   Slattery, Richard G. 1946. "A Prehistoric Indian Site on Seldon Island, Montgomery County, Maryland." *Journal of the Washington Academy of Sciences* 36:262–66.   (9)

[169]   Speck, Frank Gouldsmith. 1915. "Family Hunting Band as the Basis of Algonkian Social Organization." *American Anthropologist* 17:289–305.   (44)

[170]   ———. 1915. "The Nanticoke Community of Delaware." *Contributions from the Museum of the American Indian, Heye*

Foundation 2(4). New York: Museum of the American Indian, Heye Foundation.   (22, 29, 31, 51)

[171]   ———. 1927. *The Nanticoke and Conoy Indians with a Review of Linguistic Material from Manuscript and Living Sources: An Historical Study.* Wilmington: Historical Society of Delaware.   (22, 46)

[172]   ———. 1941. *Gourds of the Southeastern Indians: A Prolegomenon on the Lagenaria Gourd in the Culture of the Southeastern Indians.* Boston: New England Gourd Society.   (31)

[173]   ———. 1942. "Back Again to Indian River, Its People and Their Games." *Bulletin of the Archaeological Society of Delaware* 3:17–24.   (51)

[174]   ———. 1943. "The Frolic among the Nanticoke of Indian River Hundred, Delaware." *Bulletin of the Archaeological Society of Delaware* 4:2–4.   (51)

[175]   ———. 1945. "The Memorial Brush Heap in Delaware and Elsewhere." *Bulletin of the Archaeological Society of Delaware* 4:17–23.   (51)

[176]   ———. 1946. "'Cudgelling Rabbits,' an Old Nanticoke Hunting Tradition and Its Significance." *Bulletin of the Archaeological Society of Delaware* 4:9–12.   (51)

[177]   ———. 1947. "A Maker of Eel-Pots among the Nanticokes of Delaware." *Bulletin of the Archaeological Society of Delaware* 4:25–27.   (31, 51)

[178]   Stearns, Richard E. 1940. "The Hughes Site: An Aboriginal Village Site on the Potomac River in Montgomery County, Maryland." *Proceedings of the Natural History Society of Maryland,* vol. 6.   (9)

[179]   ———. 1943. "Some Indian Village Sites of Tidewater Maryland." *Proceedings of the Natural History Society of Maryland,* vol. 9.   (9)

[180]   Steiner, Bernard C. 1904. *Descriptions of Maryland.* Johns Hopkins University Studies in Historical and Political Science 11–12. Baltimore: Johns Hopkins University Press. Reprinted, New York: Johnson Reprint, 1973.   (37)

[181] Stephenson, Robert L. 1959. *The Prehistoric People of Accokeek Creek*. Accokeek, Md.: Alice Ferguson Foundation. (19, 24)

[182] ———. 1971. "The Accokeek Creek Site: Early and Middle Woodland Summary." In *Foundations of Pennsylvania Prehistory*, ed. Barry Kent, pp. 241–59. Harrisburg: Pennsylvania Historical and Museum Commission. (19)

[183] Stephenson, Robert L., Alice L. L. Ferguson, and Henry G. Ferguson. 1963. *The Accokeek Creek Site: A Middle Atlantic Seaboard Culture Sequence*. Anthropological Papers, Museum of Anthropology, University of Michigan 20. Ann Arbor: University of Michigan. (24)

[184] Stottnero-Montero, Myriam. 1963. "The Rights of the Indians in America and the English Land Policies in the Seventeenth Century Colonies in America." M.A. thesis, University of Virginia. (42)

[185] Strandberg, Carl H. 1962. "Ancient Indian Fishtraps in the Potomac River." *Photogrammetric Engineering* 28:476–78. (29)

[186]   Strandberg, Carl H., and Ray Tomlinson.
1969. "Photoarchaeological Analysis of
Potomac River Fish Traps." *American
Antiquity* 34:312–19.   (29)

[187]   Swanton, John R. 1952. *The Indian
Tribes of North America.* United States
Bureau of American Ethnology Bulle-
tin 145. Washington, D.C.: Smithsonian
Institution. Reprinted, Grosse Pointe,
Mich.: Scholarly, 1968; Washington,
D.C.: Smithsonian Institution, 1974.   (21, 34)

[188]   Tantaquidgeon, Gladys. 1942. *A Study
of Delaware Indian Medicine Practices and
Folk Beliefs.* Harrisburg: Pennsylvania
Historical and Museum Commission.
Reprinted as *Folk Medicine of the Dela-
ware and Related Algonkian Indians.*
Harrisburg: Pennsylvania Historical
and Museum Commission, 1972.   (30, 52)

[189]   Thomas, Ronald A. 1970. "Adena In-
fluence in the Middle Atlantic Coast."
In *Adena: The Seeking of an Identity,* ed.
B. K. Swartz, pp. 56–87. Muncie, Ind.:
Ball State University Press.   (10)

[190]   ———. 1976. "A Brief Survey of Prehistoric Man on the Delmarva Peninsula." In *Transactions of the Delaware Academy of Science*, vols. 5–6, ed. John C. Kraft, pp. 119–40. Newark: Delaware Academy of Science.   (14)

[191]   ———. 1976. "Webb Phase Mortuary Customs at the Island Field Site." In *Transactions of the Delaware Academy of Science*, ed. John C. Kraft, pp. 49–61. Newark: Delaware Academy of Science.   (10)

[192]   Thomas, Ronald A., Daniel R. Griffith, Cara L. Wise, and Richard E. Artusy. 1975. "Environmental Adaptation on Delaware's Coastal Plain." *Archaeology of Eastern North America* 3:35–90.   (27)

[193]   Thomas, Ronald A., and Nancy A. Warren. 1970. "A Middle Woodland Cemetery in Central Delaware: Excavations at the Island Field Site." *Bulletin of the Archaeological Society of Delaware*, n.s., vol, 8.   (10)

[194]   Tierney, Richard H. 1921. "Father Andrew White, S.J., and the Indians."

United States Catholic Historical Society, Historical Records and Studies 15:89–103.   (40)

[195]   Trigger, Bruce G., ed. 1978. *Northeast.* Vol. 15 of *Handbook of North American Indians,* gen. ed. William C. Sturtevant. 20 vols. Washington, D.C.: Government Printing Office for the Smithsonian Institution, 1978–.   (22)

[196]   Ubelaker, Douglas H. 1974. "Reconstruction of Demographic Profiles from Ossuary Skeletal Samples: A Case Study from the Tidewater Potomac." *Smithsonian Contributions to Anthropology,* vol. 18.   (36)

[197]   ———. 1976. "The Sources and Methodology for Mooney's Estimates of North American Indian Populations." In *The Native Population of the Americas in 1492,* ed. William M. Denevan, pp. 243–88. Madison: University of Wisconsin Press.   (33)

[198]   Voegelin, Charles F., and Erminie W. Voegelin. 1946. "Linguistic Considerations of Northeastern North

America." In *Man in Northeastern North America,* ed. Frederick Johnson, pp. 178–94. Andover, Mass.: Phillips Academy. (17)

[199] Wallace, Anthony F. C. 1948. "Recent Field Studies of the River Culture of the Nanticoke Indians." *Bulletin of the Philadelphia Anthropological Society* 1:3. (52)

[200] ———. 1957. "Political Organization and Land Tenure among the Northeastern Indians, 1600–1830." *Southwestern Journal of Anthropology* 13:301–27. (44)

[201] Walsh, Richard, and William Lloyd Fox, ed. 1974. *Maryland—A History.* Baltimore: Maryland Historical Society. (5)

[202] Weslager, Clinton A. 1941. "A Discussion of the Family Hunting Territory Question in Delaware." Bound with Leon de Valinger, *Indian Land Sales in Delaware.* Wilmington: Wilmington Press for the Archaeological Society of Delaware. See [38]. (xiv, 45)

[203]   ———.1942. "Indian Tribes of the Delmarva Peninsula." *Bulletin of the Archaeological Society of Delaware* 3:25–36.   (20)

[204]   ———. 1942. "Ossuaries on the Delmarva Peninsula and Exotic Influences
in the Coastal Aspect of the Woodland
Pattern." *American Antiquity* 8:142–51.   (10)

[205]   ———. 1943. *Delaware's Forgotten Folk:
The Story of the Moors and Nanticokes.*
Philadelphia: University of Pennsylvania Press.   (22, 31,
49, 52)

[206]   ———. 1944. *Delaware's Buried Past: A
Story of Archaeological Adventure.*
Philadelphia: University of Pennsylva-
nia Press. Reprinted, New Brunswick,
N.J.: Rutgers University Press, 1968.   (xiii)

[207]   ———. 1944. "Wynicaco—A Choptank Chief." *Proceedings of the American
Philosophical Society* 87:398–402.   (22, 26)

[208]   ———. 1945. "Nanticokes and the
Buzzard Song." *Bulletin of the Archaeological Society of Delaware* 4:14–17.   (52)

[209] ———. 1947. "The Anthropological Position of the Indian Tribes of the Delmarva Peninsula." *Bulletin of the Archaeological Society of Delaware* 4:3–7. (20)

[210] ———. 1947. "The Non-food Use of Corn in the Domestic Economy of the Eastern Indians." *Delaware County Institute of Science Proceedings* 10:3–22. (28)

[211] ———. 1948. *The Nanticoke Indians: A Refugee Tribal Group of Pennsylvania.* Harrisburg: Pennsylvania Historical and Museum Commission. (22, 46)

[212] ———. 1950. "Indian Tribes of the Eastern Shore of Maryland and Virginia." In *The Eastern Shore of Maryland and Virginia,* ed. Charles B. Clark, pp. 36–39. Wilmington and New York: Lewis Historical Publishing Company. (5, 20)

[213] ———. 1955. "Folklore among the Nanticokes of Indian River Hundred and the Moors of Cheswold, Delaware." *Delaware Folklore Bulletin* 1(March):17–18. (52)

[214]   ———. 1961. *The Accomac and Accohan-nock Indians from Early Relations.* Painter, Va.: Eastern Shore of Virginia Historical Society.   (26)

[215]   ———. 1963. "Folkways of the Nanticokes." *Delaware Folklore Bulletin* 1(October):37–38.   (52)

[216]   ———. 1972. *The Delaware Indians, A History.* New Brunswick: Rutgers University Press.   (26)

[217]   ———. 1973. *Magic Medicines of the Indians.* Somerset, N.J.: Middle Atlantic Press. See chapter 9, "Nanticoke and 'Moor' Medicines."   (30)

[218]   ———. 1975. "More about the Unalachtigo." *Pennsylvania Archaeologist* 45:40–44.   (22)

[219]   ———. 1978. *The Delawares: A Critical Bibliography.* Newberry Library Center for the History of the American Indian Bibliographical Series. Bloomington and London: Indiana University Press. (26)

[220]   [White, Andrew, S.J.]. 1634. *A Relation of the Successful Beginnings of the Lord Baltemore's Plantation in Maryland; Being an Extract of Certaine Letters Written from Thence, by Some of the Adventurers to Their Friends in England.* London: Anno Domini. Reprinted, Albany: J. Munsell, 1865.   (3)

[221]   White, Andrew, S.J. 1635. *A Relation of Maryland; Together with a Map of the Countrey, the Conditions of Plantation, His Majesties Charter to Lord Baltemore.* London: Anno Domini for William Peasley. Reprinted, with a prefatory note and appendix by Francis L. Hawks, New York: J. Sabin, 1865. Reprint of original ed., New York: Johnson, 1976; Amsterdam: Theatrum Orbis Terrarum, 1976.   (3)

[222]   Wilkins, Elwood S. 1976. "The Lithics of the Delaware and Nanticoke Indians." In *Transactions of the Delaware Academy of Science,* vols. 5–6, ed. John C. Kraft, pp. 25–35. Newark: Delaware Academy of Science.   (30)

[223]   Wilson, Thomas. 1899. "Chipped Stone

Classification." In *Report of the United States National Museum for 1897*, pp. 887–944. Washington, D.C.: United States National Museum.   (7)

[224] Wise, Cara L. 1971. *A Handbook for Delmarva Archaeology*. Dover, Del.: Office of Archaeology, Division of Archives and Cultural Affairs.   (14, 30)

[225] Wise, Jennings C. 1911. *Ye Kingdome of Accawmacke; or, The Eastern Shore of Virginia in the Seventeenth Century*. Richmond: Bell Book and Stationery Company. Reprinted, Baltimore: Regional Publishing Company, 1967.   (5)

[226] Witkop, C. J., C. J. MacLean, D. J. Schmidt, and J. L. Henry. 1966. "Medical and Dental Findings in the Brandywine Isolate." *Alabama Journal of Medical Sciences* 3:383–403.   (53)

[227] Wright, Henry T. 1973. *An Archaeological Sequence in the Middle Chesapeake Region*. Baltimore: Maryland Geological Survey.   (12)

[228] Wroth, Lawrence C. 1922. *A History of Printing in Colonial Maryland, 1686–1776*. Baltimore: Typothetae. Reprinted, Ann Arbor: Xerox University Microfilms, 1975. (1)

[229] ———. 1970. *The Voyages of Giovanni da Verrazzano, 1524–1528*. New Haven: Yale University Press. (37)

[230] Yap, Angelita Q. 1961. *A Study of a Kinship System: Its Structural Principles*. Washington, D.C.: Catholic University of America Press. (53)

The Newberry Library
Center for the History of the American Indian
Founding Director: D'Arcy McNickle
Director: Francis Jennings

Established in 1972 by the Newberry Library, in conjunction with the Committee on Institutional Cooperation of eleven midwestern universities, the Center makes the resources of one of America's foremost research libraries in the Humanities available to those interested in improving the quality and effectiveness of teaching American Indian history. The Newberry's collections include some 100,000 volumes on the history of the American Indian and offer specialized resources for studying historical aspects of Indian-White relations and Indian linguistics. The Center also assists Native Americans engaged in writing tribal histories and developing educational materials.

ADVISORY COMMITTEE

Chairman: Alfonso Ortiz
University of New Mexico